A HISTORY

Revolution and Restoration
England in the 1650s

A HISTORY TODAY BOOK

Revolution and Restoration
England in the 1650s

EDITED BY JOHN MORRILL

COLLINS & BROWN

Jacket illustration: This Tory/High Church
print of 1709 shows the extent to which
the issues at the heart of the
English Revolution were still the
stuff of politics decades later.
(*British Museum*)

First published in Great Britain in 1992
by Collins & Brown Limited
Mercury House
195 Knightsbridge
London SW7 1RE

A CIP catalogue record for this book
is available from the British Library

ISBN 1 85585 137 7

Typeset by Falcon Graphic Art Ltd, Wallington, Surrey
Printed and bound in Great Britain by Hartnolls Limited, Cornwall

Contents

Preface

This book was planned as a companion and sequel to *The Impact of the English Civil War*, which I edited in the same History Today series and which was published in May 1991. This new volume was commissioned, written and handed in to the publishers over a period of less than twelve months and I am deeply grateful to all the contributors for their engagement, professionalism and good-natured co-operation.

I said the following to those I asked to write for the volume:

> A tidal wave hits a coastal town. Some important buildings are destroyed, and many more are damaged, some seriously. Some of those need to be pulled down, but many are in due course repaired. Those buildings which were destroyed are eventually rebuilt in much the same style. Meanwhile the tidal wave leaves behind a new inland lake which subtly changes the eco-system. Is this a helpful metaphor for what happened to England in and after 1649?

The authors of the essays that follow have all borne that brief in mind. They are concerned to look at how irreversible changes were triggered by the events of the 1640s; and also how a process of restoration long preceded the specific Restoration of monarchy in 1660. They have concentrated on the 1650s, but have all offered some suggestions as to the long-term consequences of the Revolution. Although I have tried to ensure that each author keeps to his or her own brief and that there is little or no overlap or repetition, I have not tried to impose any consistency in the answers given to the task set. I hope the result is a book that raises issues in a lively way, and stimulates those who read it to debate these issues among themselves. We are the product of a history which has left a residue of the traumas of the 1650s in our national psyche.

November 1991   JOHN MORRILL

Introduction

JOHN MORRILL

I

In the centuries between the Norman Conquest and 30 January 1649, England had had twenty-five monarchs. Four of them had been deposed and murdered, and two others had died a violent death. But it had never occurred to anyone before the 1640s that a king could be put on trial for treason against his subjects, or that he could be executed as a criminal; and it certainly had not occurred to anyone who mattered that monarchy itself could or should be abolished.

According to the indictment laid against him on 20 January, Charles I was said to have 'traiterously and maliciously levied war against the present Parliament and the people therein represented'. It listed the main battles of the Civil War as a result of which 'much innocent blood of the free people of this nation hath been spilt [and] many families have been undone'; and it accused the King of calling on foreigners and especially on rebels in Ireland to further his cause. It concluded: 'Charles Stuart hath been, and is the occasioner, author, and continuer of the said unnatural, cruel and bloody wars; and therein guilty of all the treasons, murders, rapines, burnings, spoils, desolations, damages and mischiefs of this nation.'

Charles had to be tried for crimes recognized at common law. But those in the Army and their allies in Parliament who determined to destroy him were probably less concerned about his crimes against his people than about his crimes against God. They were convinced that by renewing the Civil War in 1648 Charles was seeking to overturn the judgement of God in giving the parliamentary forces victory in the first Civil War. Charles was committing sacrilege; he was, in the words of the Old Testament, a 'Man of Blood' who was fully responsible for the deaths of many of God's chosen people; and, according to the Old Testament, God demanded judgement against a Man of Blood. The Army saw itself as the instrument of that judgement (just as it was later to see itself as the instrument of divine retribution on the Irish people for their alleged atrocities against Irish Protestants). It was this moral outrage that made the Army dare to do what had hitherto been unthinkable.

The Regicide was the act of a desperate minority. Only one in ten of all MPs endorsed the trial and sentence, and the proportion of Parliament's supporters in the country, themselves a minority in all social groups, cannot have been any higher. By 1648 most men and women yearned for settlement, for a return to normality, and

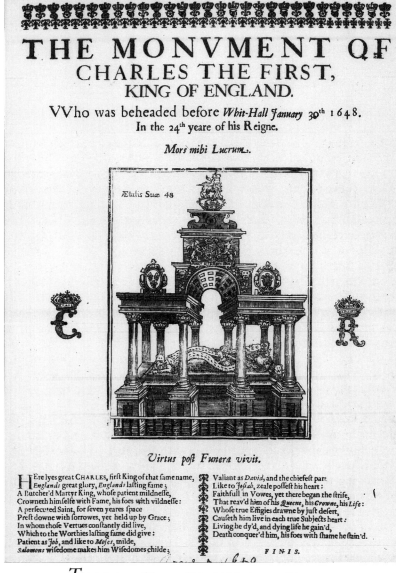

THE MONVMENT QF
CHARLES THE FIRST,
KING OF ENGLAND.

VVho was beheaded before *Whit-Hall January* 30ᵗʰ 1648.
In the 24ᵗʰ yeare of his Reigne.

Mors mihi Lucrum.

Ætatis Suæ 48

Virtus post Funera vivit.

HEre lyes great CHARLES, first King of that same name,
Englands great glory, *Englands* lasting fame;
A Butcher'd Martyr King, whose patient mildnesse,
Crowneth himselfe with Fame, his foes with vildnesse:
A persecuted Saint, for seven yeares space
Prest downe with sorrowes, yet held up by Grace;
In whom those Vertues constantly did live,
Which to the Worthies lasting fame did give:
Patient as *Job*, and like to *Moses*, milde,
Salomons wisedome makes him Wisedomes childe;

Valiant as *David*, and the chiefest part
Like to *Josiah*, zeale possest his heart:
Faithfull in Vowes, yet there began the strife,
That reav'd him of his *Queene*, his *Crowne*, his *Life*:
Whose true Effigies drawne by just desert,
Causeth him live in each true Subjects heart:
Living he dy'd, and dying life he gain'd,
Death conquer'd him, his foes with shame he stain'd.

FINIS.

*This is just one of the pamphlets which kept up royalist pressure on
the republican regime in the years after Charles I's execution by
keeping fresh the memory of a king portrayed as a virtuous martyr.*

even most of the Members of the Long Parliament had come to
believe that the war had brought nothing but chaos and confusion
in its wake. Any deal with the King was better than none. Only
in the New Model Army, with its extraordinary belief in itself as
a body called forth by God to serve His cause, an army undefeated

in four years, did another feeling predominate. Many in the Army, spearheaded by its second-in-command, Oliver Cromwell, believed that all the suffering, all the bloodshed, the very descent into chaos was all part of a divine plan, that God's overturning of the corruptions of the past was a clearing of the way for Him to do great things with and for his new chosen people, the English.

II

The events of January 1649 constitute a truly revolutionary moment. The abolition of monarchy, the abolition of the House of Lords, the closely linked abolition of the Church of England and of the principle that all men and women ought to be members of a single national Church, represent the destruction of those very institutions around which men and women organized their view of the natural order in the world. No wonder there quickly emerged groups who believed that the end of the world was nigh, that Jesus himself was about to return to preside over a 1,000-year rule of the saints culminating in the Day of Judgement and the end of time; groups who believed that the overthrow of kings prefigured the end of private property and a return to a world in which the world became a common treasury shared equally by all. Intellectuals like John Milton were so liberated by the sense of the institutions they had taken for granted tumbling around them that they challenged the most basic moral values of their society – in Milton's case by pleading for Christian divorce and against the most basic of religious teachings, such as the divinity of Christ and the doctrine of the Trinity. The unthinkable act of Regicide freed men to think unthinkable thoughts.

Among other things it led to that series of radical groups that so preoccupied contemporaries and have so preoccupied recent historians: Levellers, Diggers, Ranters, Fifth Monarchists, Muggletonians, Quakers. Varying in size and in the degree to which they genuinely sought to turn the world upside down, these groups have too often been seen as a series of discrete movements. This leads to difficulties in classifying the likes of Lawrence Clarkson, successively Anglican, Presbyterian, Independent, Baptist, Seeker, Ranter and Muggletonian. It is worth considering the recent suggestion of Jonathan Scott that we should see these groups not as a series of *movements* but as a succession of *moments*. He suggests we abandon seeking to recruit members to a range of radical 'organizations' and witness 'a single process by which the nature of radical expectations changed in response to changing external events': the Leveller moment, as men and women sought to reclaim their natural rights by overthrowing all the tyrannies of the present and establishing a more just political order for the future; a Fifth Monarchist moment anticipating that the Second Coming of King Jesus would free mankind from the thraldom of sinful nature; and a Quaker moment, a disillusionment with the capacity of worldly agencies to deliver, and a turning to the inner voice, the Temple of Grace, to sanctify the troubled soul in an irredeemably broken and fallen world.

This image is of Cromwell as the all-conquering soldier. A caption lists over 300 victories he secured between the outset of the civil wars and his return from Ireland in June 1650.

These secretaries are the most eloquent and the most subversive witnesses to the new freedom made possible by the Revolution. They quickly tried the patience of those who had fought for religious liberty but who saw the sects as turning that liberty to licence, in much the same way as the libertarian opponents of censorship in the 1960s have recoiled as child pornographers and racists have claimed a right to peddle their ideas in the name of that liberty.

Oliver Cromwell was the epitome of the Puritan Revolution. He was a man liberated from the constraints of ancient constitutionalism and of ecclesiastical strait–jackets. But he was also a man who found that those he freed to find their own way to obey God were cruelly abusing that freedom. Liberty was turned to licentiousness and the freedom of the saints degenerated into the malice of the self-righteous.

Nothing illustrates Cromwell's disillusionment so much as the contrast between his chiding of his first Parliament for standing by while 'there is yet upon the spirits of men a strange itch; nothing will satisfy them unless they can press their fingers upon their brethren's conscience to pinch them there', and his bitter and exhausted outburst just three years later: 'we have an appetite to variety – to be not only making wounds but widening those already made. As if you should see one making wounds in a man's side and eager only to be groping and grovelling with his fingers in those wounds. They will be making wounds and rending and tearing and making them wider.' In killing King Charles, Cromwell believed that God had called him to rebuild Zion. Instead he came to fear that he had merely rebuilt the Tower of Babel.

III

While the 1650s was a decade rich in new ideas and in rhetoric, it was arguably much less rich in solid achievement. Those who cut off the King's head in a sense cut themselves off from past-rootedness, from ancient constitutionalism. Nothing was more a part of the immemorial past than kingship. Nothing, said the silver-tongued lawyers who tempted Cromwell with the offer of the Crown in 1657, was so likely to promote peace and settlement as the restoration of the kingly office: 'the new title, that of Protector, was not known to the law; that of King is, and has been for many hundreds of years. It will ground itself in all the ancient foundations of the laws of England.' In large part Cromwell turned down the offer precisely because it would restrict his freedom of action. He would be bound to and by the wisdom of the past. But if he could not seek to legitimize himself by appealing to the past, nor could he – however much he would have liked to do so – legitimize himself by an appeal to the present. He could never claim to be governing by consent. For the Interregnum was created by acts of violence – the military putsch of 6 December 1648 known as Pride's Purge followed by the Regicide – and successive regimes were sustained only by shows of force. It was the Army that launched almost all the experiments of the period and used demonstrations of force in 1653, 1659 and 1660 to remove experiments it did not like. The regimes of the 1650s, in Christopher Hill's evocative phrase, were therefore all 'sitting on bayonets'. There were no free elections between 1640 and the summer of 1661: in the elections of 1654, 1656, 1659 and 1660 there were political tests limiting the right to vote and the right to stand as a candidate and more than a quarter of those elected were forcibly excluded from both Oliver Cromwell's parliaments. Any Parliament freely elected on traditional franchises in the 1650s would have recalled Charles II, restored the House of Lords and (less certainly) re-established much if not all of the Elizabethan Church settlement. Cromwell was endlessly torn between seeing the Revolution as being a liberation of the people of God – the saints – and a call to the English nation as a new chosen race, He oscillated between using the godly to herd the 'fleshly' majority along, and seeking ways to work with the whole people as the elect nation. 'I would all the Lord's people were prophets. It ought to be the longing of your hearts to see all men fit to be called,' he told the Nominated Assembly in 1653. Ultimately, however, he is at his most self-revealing when he asserted that 'Government is for the people's good, not what pleases them.' Consent was desirable but not attainable.

Cromwell was thus cut off from appeals to the past and to the present. He sought to justify himself and the Revolution he led by appeals to a glorious future. It was this that made him so preoccupied with ends and not with means, and this in turn justified his disregard for civil rights whenever anyone or anything stood in the way of the fulfilment of what he took to be God's purpose. In 1653, Cromwell spoke of the English nation being on 'the edge of promises and prophecies'. He recalled psalm 68: 'there it prophesies that "He will bring His people again from the depths of the Sea, as once He led Israel through the Red Sea." God will set up the glory of the Gospel Church, it shall be a gathering of the people "out of deep waters", "out of the multitude of the waters", such are His people drawn out of the multitudes of the nations and people of the world.' His commitment was to building a new and godly order. We have already seen how he was to die an exhausted and disillusioned man. By 1660, the cause he led was exhausted and disillusioned too.

The Interregnum was, then, a vanguard state, a succession of revolutionary regimes that governed for, but not by the will of, the people. It was characterized by a determination to compel all men to accept the responsibilities of freedom made possible by the destruction of old tyrannies. The circumstances of its creation, the sheer cost of maintaining the Army which remained its guarantor, the itch to make people use their freedom in ways that few felt drawn to, all these things doomed successive regimes to a tenuous hold on power. The social conservatism and the commitment to the agenda of moral reformation characteristic of convinced Calvinists (strict sexual codes, strict sabbatarianism, the active discouragement of the culture of the alehouse and the village green) only increased a roseate memory of more permissive times. It was the good old days not the Good Old Cause which gained ground in the 1650s. Yet as the debt-ridden Republic stumbled along in 1659–60 and as the Army splintered into deadly fragments, we find that it was the Church of England that came back, even before the Crown. Charles II was proclaimed on 8 May 1660, but three weeks earlier Easter Day – a festival proscribed in 1644 – was celebrated in two-thirds of English parishes.

One incident – typical of many – sums it all up. Adam Martindale had been a labourer in the Lord's vineyard in Rostherne (Cheshire) since 1647. He had preached to, catechized and cherished his flock. He had been a caring and not a severe pastor. On May morning 1660,

*Although most former parliamentarians were pardoned at the
Restoration, ten were hideously executed and the corpses of Cromwell,
Ireton and Bradshaw were disinterred and publicly displayed.*

Martindale found that local youths, urged on by some of their elders,
had erected a maypole near the church. He strode off to church and
denounced the maypole 'as a relic of the shameful worship of the
strumpet of Rome'. His wife – more stridently – 'assisted with three
young women, whipt it down in the night[time] with a framing saw.
This made them almost mad, and put them to the trouble of piecing it
[together] with another pole.' Martindale took such comfort from the
episode as he could; but its real lesson is the futility and self-defeating
toils of the Puritan activists.

With the return of the King, there was an explicit, even obses-
sive, concern to return to the past, to root everything in ancient
constitutionalism. And although perhaps five per cent of the population harboured more or less open resentments, the dominant mood
was that civil war must never happen again. It is hard to deny that
the Puritan drive that had been the motor of the Revolution stalled
in 1660. Or, to put it another way, the Revolution proved a curious
kind of Cheshire cat: it vanished, leaving only a scowl behind.

CHAPTER I

The Struggle for New Constitutional and Institutional Forms

DAVID L. SMITH

I

On 8 May 1660, the Convention Parliament declared Charles II to have been 'undoubted King' from the moment of his father's execution on 30 January 1649. The Interregnum had technically never existed, and officially no time had elapsed between Regicide and Restoration. It was as if a clock had been stopped in 1649, only to be restarted in 1660. But historically, of course, the clock did not stop. In reality, eleven troubled and turbulent years separated Charles I's death from his son's triumphant return. These years witnessed a bewildering array of constitutional experiments, of new and sometimes bizarre institutions intended to provide stable

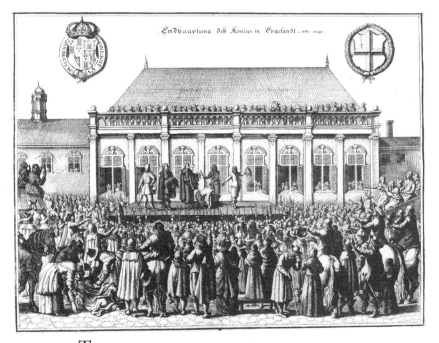

This contemporary Dutch depiction of Charles I's execution outside the Banqueting House in Whitehall graphically portrays the public's stunned horror; and contrasts the coats of arms of the defeated monarchy and the fledgeling Commonwealth.

and godly government. Yet, one by one, each experiment collapsed; and in 1660 they were obliterated without trace.

In this essay, I shall argue that the essence of the problem lay in the incompatibility of the 'godly commonwealth' sought by the Army, and the return to stability and tradition which the majority of those involved in politics desired. Between 1649 and 1660, no republican regime could survive without the Army's backing; yet equally, no civilian politicians could fulfil the Army's expectations for long. A national referendum held at any stage between 1649 and 1660 would have restored the monarchy with a massive majority, and the Army would have been disbanded. Faced with such popular conservatism, the soldiers and politicians of the Interregnum needed each other, yet could not work harmoniously together. That paradox is the key to understanding why their institutional experiments failed to generate stability.

II

The first experiment, which lasted from January 1649 until April 1653, might be termed 'rule by dismembered Parliament'. In December 1648, the Army had 'purged' the Long Parliament to prevent its reaching a settlement with Charles I. Colonel Pride's troops arrested 45 MPs and prevented another 186 from taking their seats, while a further 86 withdrew in protest. Then, on 4 January 1649, the remaining 'Rump' of the Commons declared that it possessed 'the supreme power in this nation', and that 'whatever' it 'enacted' had 'the force of law' even without the consent of King and Lords. This claim provided the justification for the Rump's creation of a High Court of Justice to try the King; and for its exercise of sovereignty over the ensuing four and a quarter years. With the Army's blessing, supreme power passed from King, Lords and Commons to a purged fragment of the Commons.

Following the execution of the King, the Rump abolished the House of Lords (6 February 1649) and the monarchy (7 February) as 'useless' and 'dangerous' to the people of England. On 13 February the executive functions of monarchy were vested in a Council of State, to be elected annually by MPs and predominantly from among MPs. Then, on 19 May, the Rump passed an act declaring England 'to be a Commonwealth and Free State'. Henceforth, 'the supreme authority of this nation' lay with 'the representatives of the people in Parliament . . . and that without any King or House of Lords'. Finally, on 17 July 1650, anyone who claimed that 'the Commons in Parliament [were] not the supreme authority' was 'adjudged' guilty of 'high treason', a crime which hitherto could only be committed against a reigning monarch. With this Treason Act, the transfer of sovereignty to the remnant of the Long Parliament was complete.

What use did the Rump make of these sweeping powers? The evidence tells a story of dwindling energy, growing lethargy and unfulfilled promise. Several statistics are stark illustrations of this. About 210 MPs sat in Parliament at some stage between January

Table of main constitutional events, 1649–60

30 January 1649	Execution of Charles I
6 February 1649	Abolition of the House of Lords
7 February 1649	Abolition of the monarchy
13 February 1649	Council of State appointed
19 May 1649	England declared a 'Commonwealth'
17 July 1650	Treason Act
12 August 1652	Act for the Settlement of Ireland
20 April 1653	Cromwell dissolves the Rump Parliament
4 July 1653	The Nominated Assembly assembles
12 December 1653	The Nominated Assembly surrenders power to Cromwell
15 December 1653	The Instrument of Government adopted
16 December 1653	Cromwell installed as Lord Protector
12 April 1654	Act for Union with Scotland
27 June 1654	Acts for Elections in Scotland and Ireland
3 September 1654	First Protectorate Parliament assembles
22 January 1655	Cromwell dissolves first Protectorate Parliament
11 October 1655	Instructions to the Major-Generals
2 November 1655	Major-Generals begin to work in localities
17 September 1656	Second Protectorate Parliament assembles
28 January 1657	Decimation Tax and Major-Generals abandoned
23 February 1657	Offer of the kingship to Cromwell
21 April 1657	Cromwell's refusal of the kingship
25 May 1657	*The Humble Petition and Advice* adopted
4 February 1658	Cromwell dissolves second Protectorate Parliament
3 September 1658	Death of Oliver Cromwell
27 January 1659	Third Protectorate Parliament assembles
22 April 1659	Third Protectorate Parliament dissolved
7 May 1659	Rump Parliament re-assembles
24 May 1659	Resignation of Richard Cromwell
13 October 1659	Army expels the Rump Parliament
27 October 1659	Committee of Safety established
17 December 1659	Committee of Safety disperses
27 December 1659	Rump Parliament re-assembles
21 February 1660	Monck secures re-admission of MPs 'purged' in December 1648
16 March 1660	Long Parliament calls 'free elections' and dissolves itself
4 April 1660	Charles II's Declaration of Breda
25 April 1660	Convention Parliament assembles
8 May 1660	Convention Parliament declares Charles II to have been King since 30 January 1649
29 May 1660	Charles II enters London

1649 and April 1653; but only between 60 and 70 of these were at all active, and the average attendance was between 50 and 60. The number of acts passed by the Rump fell steadily: 125 in 1649; 78 in 1650; 54 in 1651; 44 in 1652; 10 between 1 January and 20 April 1653. The number of committees appointed to prepare legislation declined even more steeply: 152 in 1649; 98 in 1650; 61 in 1651; 51 in 1652; 12 between 1 January and 20 April 1653. The nature of the Rump's legislation likewise indicates that zeal for radical reform rapidly petered out. Of a representative sample of the 131 acts passed in January–May 1649, January–May 1651 and 1 January–20 April 1653, 74 dealt with matters of security, finance or taxation; 43 with local government or the Army; and 14 with social problems. Only 5 addressed religious matters; 3 law reform; and 6 economic or social reforms. By 1652–3, the Rump was drifting from day to day, totally without appetite for positive, creative reform.

To the Army leaders, and especially to the Lord General Oliver Cromwell, this was quite intolerable. The Council of Officers had hoped that the Rump would 'proceed vigorously in reforming what was amiss in government, and to the settling of the Commonwealth upon a foundation of justice and righteousness'. Instead came the

'You have sat here too long for the good you do': Cromwell denounces and then dissolves the Rump Parliament, 20 April 1653. Yet later Parliaments proved no better able to realize his vision of a 'godly commonwealth'.

sickening realization that 'this Parliament . . . would never answer those ends which God, His people, and the whole nation expected from them'. Under Army pressure, the Rump finally agreed to dissolve itself on 3 November 1653.

But what would replace it? The Army was in no doubt: England's rulers had to be 'pious and faithful to the interest of the Commonwealth'. Hence, when the Rump voted on 20 April 1653 to hold fresh elections, without any mechanism for 'screening' candidates, Cromwell led a company of troops to Westminster, castigated the Rumpers as 'whoremasters' and 'drunkards', and forcibly expelled them. Two days later, he declared – almost certainly incorrectly – that the Rump had wished to 'perpetuate themselves'. But his underlying fear was probably that any assembly returned by free elections would be even less committed to godly reform than the Rump. At any rate, he insisted that 'the interest of all honest men and of this glorious cause had been in danger to be laid in the dust', and that 'necessity and providence' had compelled him to terminate the Rump's 'misgovernment of affairs'. The last vestige of the Long Parliament was thus destroyed, and supreme power passed to Lord General Cromwell and his Council of Officers.

III

Then followed what was perhaps the most radical experiment of the 1650s. Believing that the Rump had betrayed the godly, the Army now devised a Parliament *consisting of* the godly. This institution, based on the ancient Jewish Sanhedrin or assembly of 'saints', was unique in English constitutional history. The brainchild of Major-General Thomas Harrison, it was embraced by Cromwell as a panacea which would guarantee 'the peace, safety, and good government of this Commonwealth'. It met in an atmosphere of unparalleled optimism and euphoria; yet it lasted less than six months.

Its members were chosen in a totally different way from any other Parliament before or since. The Army officers, taking up and building on nominations sent in by separatist congregations such as Baptist or Fifth Monarchist churches, selected 139 'persons fearing God, and of approved fidelity and honesty'; men, as Cromwell put it, 'with the root of the matter in them'. A further five members, including Cromwell and Harrison, were later co-opted. The religious zeal of this 'Nominated Assembly' – or 'Barebone's Parliament' as it came to be known – was very unusual; but the social profile of its members was not. They represented a shift of power *within* the gentry, not *away from* the gentry. At least four-fifths ranked as gentlemen; and no fewer than 119 served as JPs at some stage in their career.

When this body assembled on 4 July 1653, Cromwell welcomed it as 'a door to usher in things that God hath promised and prophesied of'. It was 'called to supreme authority' by a series of 'marvellous dispensations' and 'wonderful providences'. Cromwell concluded by assuring members that the Army would 'leave [them] to [their] own thoughts and to the guidance of God'.

'*A door to usher in things that God hath promised and prophesied of*': The Nominated Assembly met in July 1653 amid heady optimism; but within six months this bold attempt to establish 'rule by the saints' lay in ruins.

The achievements of the Nominated Assembly were far from negligible. It established fifteen committees to draft legislation, and passed a total of twenty-nine ordinances dealing with a wide range of administrative, financial and social matters. Among its most startling innovations were the requirement that all marriages be performed not by the clergy but by a Justice of the Peace; the compulsory civil registration of births, marriages and deaths within each parish; provisions for the relief of impoverished creditors and debtors; greater protection for lunatics and their estates; and tougher measures against thieves and highwaymen. However, the Assembly's combination of religious radicalism and social conservatism – which mirrored a duality within Cromwell's own nature – ultimately proved disastrous. Deep rifts soon opened up. The forty members with some legal training were greatly alarmed when it voted to abolish the ancient Court of Chancery and to codify the common law. When members elected a new Council of State on 1 November, the results showed a dramatic swing away from the radicals. Many moderates perceived the suppression of the rights of laymen to nominate the ministers of particular parishes on 17 November as an attack on property rights. The last straw came on 10 December, when a motion to abolish tithes – many of which were paid to the laity – was defeated by a tiny majority. Two days later, nearly 80 moderates, exploiting the radicals' absence from Parliament at a prayer meeting, voted 'to deliver up unto the Lord General Cromwell the powers which they received from him'. So ended the experiment with 'rule by the saints', an episode which Cromwell later called 'a story of my own weakness and folly'.

IV

It was symptomatic of the institutional fluidity of these years that the Army leaders already had an alternative constitution to hand. The *Instrument of Government* had been drafted by Major-General John Lambert in October–November 1653, and enshrined the principle of rule by 'one single person and a Parliament'. It was England's first ever paper constitution, and thus marked another dramatic departure from earlier practice.

Under the terms of the Instrument of Government, executive powers passed to an elected Lord Protector advised by a Council of State numbering between thirteen and twenty-one. Cromwell was declared Lord Protector for life, but it was stressed that his office was 'elective and not hereditary'. 'Supreme legislative authority' lay with the Lord Protector and triennial parliaments sitting for at least five months. Parliament was to consist of one chamber of 400 English and Welsh MPs, plus 30 each from Scotland and Ireland, and was to assemble for the first time on 3 September 1654. Senior public officials would be 'chosen by the approbation of Parliament'. Fifteen Councillors of State were named in the Instrument of Government; subsequent vacancies were to be filled by Parliament, or by co-option when it was not sitting. Parliament had no 'power to alter the government as it is hereby settled in one single person and a Parliament'; and until it met the Lord Protector could issue 'laws and ordinances' which were 'binding in force'. He was granted 'a constant yearly revenue' for maintaining an army of 30,000 troops, plus a further £200,000 per annum 'for defraying . . . expenses of the government'. Between them, the Lord Protector and Parliament wielded immense powers, and the effectiveness of the new constitution depended on their ability to work amicably together.

The Army's desire to promote a 'godly commonwealth' through institutional reform was also evident. MPs had to be 'persons of known integrity, fearing God, and of good conversation'. Roman Catholics and Irish rebels could neither stand nor vote, and those who had 'aided, advised, assisted, or abetted' Charles I were disqualified for twelve years. A national Church would ensure the 'public pro-

Comparative Summary of the Constitutions of England, 1649–60

	The Common-wealth	The Instrument of Government	The Humble Petition and Advice	The Restoration Settlement
Nature of constitution	Unwritten	Written	Written	Unwritten
Form of Government	Republic	Republic	Republic	Hereditary monarchy
Devised by	Rump Parliament	Army Council of Officers	Second Protectorate Parliament	Charles II working with Convention and Cavalier parliaments
Supreme executive authority	Parliament	Lord Protector elected by Parliament and advised by Council of State	Lord Protector (=Cromwell for life) advised by Privy Council	Hereditary monarch advised by Privy Council
Council	Council of State of 40 elected by Parliament	Council of State of 13–21 elected by Parliament (and by co-option between parliaments)	Privy Council of 21 chosen by Lord Protector and approved by Parliament	Privy Council chosen by the monarch
Supreme legislative authority	Ordinances issued by Parliament	Ordinances issued by Lord Protector and/or Parliament	Ordinances issued by Lord Protector and Parliament	Statutes agreed by monarch and two Houses of Parliament

fession' of 'sound doctrine', while religious 'liberty' was granted to 'such as profess faith in God by Jesus Christ', but not to 'popery', 'prelacy' or 'licentiousness'. Different forms of government; but always the same drive towards godly reformation.

The Council of Officers adopted the Instrument of Government on 15 December, and Cromwell was installed as Lord Protector in Westminster Hall the next day. Ever enthusiastic about new constitutional experiments, he issued 84 ordinances over the ensuing nine months; and when the first Protectorate Parliament met he hailed it as 'a door of hope' which would lead to 'healing and settling'. But again he was bitterly disappointed. The divergence between the Army's priorities and those of most civilian politicians became strikingly clear. Parliament did not draft a single statute, but instead drew up a series of amendments to the Instrument of Government,

	The Common-wealth	The Instrument of Government	The Humble Petition and Advice	The Restoration Settlement
Parliament	Purged 'Rump' of Long Parliament (1649–53); Nominated Assembly of 144 'saints' (1653)	Single chamber of 460 MPs, including 30 Scots and 30 Irish	House of Commons of 460 MPs; 'Other House' of 40–70 nominated by Lord Protector and approved by Commons	House of Lords containing hereditary peers and 26 bishops; freely elected House of Commons of 550 MPs
Financial settlement	*Ad hoc* fiscal measures; no overall settlement	Lord Protector to receive annual revenue for Army plus £200,000	Lord Protector to receive annual revenue of £1.3 m.	Monarch to receive annual revenue of £1.2 m.
Religious Settlement	Presbyterian State Church; toleration of Independents and sectaries; penalties against Catholics and Anglicans	National State Church with toleration for all except papists and prelatists	National State Church with toleration for all except papists and prelatists; new penalties against blasphemies	Re-established Church of England, with new penalties against Catholics and Protestant Nonconformists
Military establishment	Standing British Army of 60–65,000 troops under command of Lord General (=Cromwell)	Standing British Army of 30,000 troops under command of Lord Protector	Standing British Army of 30,000 troops under command of Lord Protector and Parliament	Standing British Army of 13–14,000 troops under command of monarch
Provision for alteration of constitution	By parliamentary ordinance	By Lord Protector, but not by Parliament	By agreement between Lord Protector and Parliament	By statutes agreed by monarchs-in-Parliament

greatly augmenting its own powers. Infuriated by its failure to make 'good and wholesome laws' which would protect 'the honest meaning people of the nation', Cromwell dissolved Parliament at the earliest possible opportunity allowed by the Instrument, on 22 January 1655. When, seven weeks later, he faced a Royalist insurrection in Wiltshire (Penruddock's Rising) he decided on more drastic measures.

V

Hitherto, the Army leaders had tried to achieve their aims through various civilian assemblies: the Rump, the Nominated Assembly, the first Protectorate Parliament. But in August 1655, they cut loose and imposed direct military rule. England and Wales were divided into 11 regions, each governed by a senior army officer. These 11 Major-Generals received detailed commissions the following October.

Their first duty was to maintain security. They were to suppress 'all tumults, insurrections, rebellions or other unlawful assemblies'; to disarm 'all papists and others who have been in arms against the Parliament'; and to apprehend all 'thieves, robbers, highwaymen and other dangerous persons'. To these ends, Cromwell authorized the Major-Generals to raise new regional militias totalling 6,000 horse, funded by the Decimation Tax, a ten per cent income tax on all former Royalists.

But the Major-Generals' instructions went far beyond this. They were to become the agents of moral reform in the localities. 'No horse-races, cock-fighting, bear-baitings, stage plays, or any unlawful assemblies' were 'permitted within their counties'. Instead, the Major-Generals were to 'encourage and promote godliness and virtue, and discourage and discountenance all profaneness and ungodliness'. They were required to enforce 'the laws against drunkenness, blaspheming and taking of the name of God in vain, by swearing and cursing, plays and interludes, and profaning the Lord's Day, and such-like wickedness and abominations'. All alehouses were to be closed 'except such as are necessary and convenient to travellers'. Cromwell sought what he termed a 'reformation of manners'.

In September 1656, Cromwell claimed that the Major-Generals had been 'more effectual towards the discountenancing of vice and settling religion than anything done these fifty years'. But modern research has suggested that their success was at best patchy. Most of the Major-Generals were from very humble backgrounds, which reduced their influence over the traditional rulers of provincial society. Some were further hampered by coming from outside the areas they ruled. Above all, the Major-Generals were a very diverse bunch, ranging from the zealous Charles Worsley (Cheshire, Lancashire, Staffordshire), who closed over 200 alehouses in his first month and eventually died of overwork, to the ineffectual William Goffe (Berkshire, Hampshire, Sussex), who repeatedly professed himself a 'poor and inconsiderable creature . . . unworthy of the employment'. The impact of the Major-Generals varied enormously from region to region.

What was common to all areas, however, was the intense unpopularity of military rule. Growing civilian pressure, especially from the legal profession, and the urgent need to finance military operations in the West Indies forced Cromwell to call a second Protectorate Parliament for 17 September 1656. The cry 'No swordsmen! No decimators!' dominated the elections, and again the results were not to the Army's liking. The Council of Officers excluded nearly 100 'ungodly' MPs on the first day, while a further 50 to 60 immediately withdrew in protest. The officers' motive was summed up by Major-General Thomas Kelsey: 'The interest of God's people is to be preferred before a thousand Parliaments.' But this purge failed to make Parliament more malleable. MPs bitterly condemned the Major-Generals and the Decimation Tax, forcing Cromwell to abandon both on 28 January 1657. They then turned to more fundamental questions. Could the Army really be trusted to respect a parliamentary constitution? Might the Lord Protector's powers lie open to abuse? Was there not a case, some MPs wondered, for 'an alteration of the present government' to remove these hazards?

VI

It is in this context that Parliament's offer of the Crown to Cromwell on 23 February 1657 should be understood. Whereas the office of king was known to the common law of England, and therefore subject to ancient legal restrictions, that of Lord Protector was not. This prompted a group of MPs to draw up a new paper constitution, known as *The Humble Petition and Advice*, which would guarantee the role of Parliament and make Cromwell king.

Cromwell now faced the most agonizing decision of his career. As early as 1651, he had mused that 'a settlement with somewhat of monarchical power in it would be very effectual'. A year later, he asked the common lawyer Bulstrode Whitelocke 'what if a man should take upon him to be King?' Yet in April 1657, after two anguished months, he refused the Crown. His motives remain highly controversial, but the likeliest explanation is that he perceived the 'fears' voiced by his Army colleagues and the 'apprehensions' of the religious radicals as signs of God's disapproval. Certainly, on 13 April he declared that 'the Providence of God hath laid aside this title of King providentially *de facto* . . . I will not set up that which Providence hath destroyed and laid in the dust; I will not build Jericho again.' There would be no King Oliver.

That decided, the other clauses of *The Humble Petition and Advice* were approved with little modification on 25 May 1657. This became England's second – and last – paper constitution. Unlike the Instrument of Government, it was drafted, amended and formally adopted by Parliament, not by the Army leaders. The result was a marked shift back towards traditional forms of government.

Cromwell was to remain Lord Protector, but could now choose his own successor. He was required to rule 'according to the laws of these nations', and to 'call Parliaments . . . once in three years'. These consisted of two chambers: a House of Commons and an 'Other House' of between forty and seventy persons 'nominated' by the Lord Protector but 'approved' by the Commons. Mindful of recent purges, Parliament demanded that its 'ancient and undoubted liberties and privileges . . . be preserved and maintained', and that the Lord Protector would not 'suffer them to be broken or interrupted'. Those 'chosen by a free election' could only be excluded 'by judgement and consent' of Parliament. In a particularly striking reversion to earlier institutions, a 'Privy Council' of no more than 21 was to be chosen by the Lord Protector and then 'approved' by Parliament. The religious settlement clearly reflected MPs' fears that 'liberty' had run to 'licence': while broadly similar to that of 1653,

'I will not build Jericho again'. Nevertheless, Cromwell was eventually King in all but name, and this contemporary engraving depicts him in ermine robes, wearing a crown, holding an orb and sceptre, and surrounded by the full trappings of monarchy.

it introduced new measures against 'blasphemies'. Finally, the Lord Protector was granted 'a yearly revenue' of £1.3 million, exclusive of land taxes. *The Humble Petition and Advice* signalled a reassertion of parliamentary government by civilian politicians, and a retreat from the summits of godly reformation scaled by the Army leaders.

That retreat was symbolized by Cromwell's second installation as Lord Protector on 26 June 1657. Whereas in December 1653 he had worn 'a plain black suit and cloak' – the austere garb of a godly squire – he now donned 'a robe of purple velvet lined with ermine' and carried a golden sceptre. He took an adapted form of the royal coronation oath, and left Westminster Hall in a 'coach of state' amid cries of 'God save the Lord Protector'. Lacking only a crown, he was now king in all but name.

Parliament then adjourned until 20 January 1658. On reconvening, it was joined by those MPs purged in 1656 and by an 'Other House' of 42. Cromwell hoped that this session would promote 'peace and tranquillity' and safeguard 'the honest and religious interest of the nation'. Instead, MPs began to question the title, rights and legitimacy of the 'Other House'. For many republicans, such as Sir Arthur Haselrig and Thomas Scot, it was too reminiscent of the House of Lords. In exasperation, Cromwell rushed to Westminster on 4 February, harangued Parliament for disappointing his 'very comfortable expectations' and declared it 'high time' that Parliament be dissolved. 'And let God,' he concluded, 'be judge between you and me.'

Cromwell called no more parliaments: broken and disillusioned, he died on 3 September 1658. An institution through which he might realize his vision of a godly commonwealth had eluded him. That vision, which he shared with many officers but few civilians, explains both his relentless search for new forms of government and his consistent failure to make them work. One quotation captures perfectly his attitude towards constitutional reform. In 1647, Cromwell asserted that he was not 'wedded and glued to forms of government', for they were 'but dross and dung in comparison of Christ'. The struggles of the next eleven years would give those words new depths of meaning and poignancy.

VII

So far, I have concentrated on developments at the centre. But what about the institutions of local government during the Interregnum? How were the English provinces administered, order maintained, taxes raised? The evidence reveals a complex blend of old and new; but the same drift back towards traditional forms and personnel.

In January 1649, the shires of England were ruled by Parliamentarian county committees. Originally created in the winter of 1642–3, these had gained unprecedented powers over provincial administration, finance and security. However, in January 1650 fiscal pressure forced the Rump to assume direct control over sequestered Royalist estates and over the 'composition' fines paid for their release. This deprived the county committees of their principal source of revenue. As a result, they withered away, and in their place older institutions – eclipsed in the 1640s – began to re-emerge.

Most of the county committees' administrative functions reverted to the commission of the peace, traditionally the lynchpin of local government. Central government made little attempt to stop this, and simply insisted that all office-holders take an 'Engagement' to be 'true and faithful to the Commonwealth of England as it is now established, without a King or House of Lords'. This requirement removed between a third and a tenth of JPs in 1650, and those who filled the vacancies mostly came from outside the established ruling families of county society. Further purges followed in many counties during 1652–3. But, from 1655–6, members of the traditional governing class steadily returned to most commissions of the peace.

Much the same was true of local justice. As the county committees disintegrated, their judicial powers returned to the ancient county courts: the Quarter Sessions, where JPs tried minor offences every three months; and the twice-yearly Assizes, when common law judges visited the shire to deal with more serious felonies. The number of cases heard by these courts increased exponentially in the majority of counties throughout the Interregnum. Most borough assemblies and courts enjoyed a comparable revival. Furthermore, this bringing together of gentry as justices and jurors promoted reconciliation between former political opponents.

A similar trend is apparent in the management of finance. Central government's two main sources of revenue during the 1650s remained the two direct taxes which Parliament had introduced in 1643: the monthly 'assessment' (a land tax) and the 'excise' (a tax on consumables such as meat, salt and beer). On average, these raised £834,573 and £395,024 a year respectively. In addition, customs dues yielded an average of £361,807 a year. This represented an unparalleled burden: at its peak, the assessment was bringing in about eighteen pre-war parliamentary subsidies a year. But here too old habits died hard. The Exchequer, England's main financial organ since the twelfth century, had effectively ground to a halt during the Civil War. But in 1654 it was reconstituted to collect and disburse all branches of revenue except the assessment. The taxes were new, but the institution which administered them was very ancient.

All these developments show that radical regimes in London were unable to alter significantly the machinery of local government. Or *unwilling*? Perhaps we should remember here that Cromwell was never a social revolutionary. In September 1654, he promised to defend 'the ranks and orders of men, whereby England hath been known for hundreds of years', and stated categorically: 'a nobleman, a gentleman, a yeoman; the distinction of these, that is a good interest of the nation, and a great one'. Such an attitude makes the survival of traditional county élites and structures under his rule easier to understand.

VIII

But this policy only applied to England: Cromwell treated Scotland and Ireland quite differently. During 1649–51 he faced a Royalist threat from both nations; and he rapidly conquered each in turn. This then raised the question of how the Scots and Irish were to be governed. Cromwell's answer – incorporative union to create a single 'Commonwealth of England, Scotland and Ireland' – was among the most radical constitutional innovations of these years.

When Charles I was beheaded, the Scots immediately proclaimed Charles II King of Scotland, and of England and Ireland as well. To remove this danger, Cromwell launched a series of campaigns against the Scots and defeated them at the battles of Dunbar (3 September 1650) and Worcester (3 September 1651). But he wanted as far as possible to 'avoid blood in this business,' for the Scots were 'a people fearing [God's] name, though deceived'.

This view of the Scots as co-religionists determined the arrangements made for their government. On 28 October 1651, the Rump drew up a declaration 'concerning the settlement of Scotland', later published in February 1652. 'For the advancement of the glory of God, and the good and welfare of the whole island,' this proclaimed, Scotland was to 'be incorporated into, and become one Commonwealth with this of England'. The lands of those in arms against the English Parliament since 1648 were to be 'confiscated and forfeited to the use and benefit of the Commonwealth of England'. However, all others who 'put themselves under the protection of' Parliament were to be 'pardoned for all acts past' and 'set free' from their former duties as vassals or tenants of landowners.

The English were anxious to portray this as an offer of union to which the Scots had voluntarily consented. But in reality the 'negotiations' during January 1652 presented Scotland with a *fait accompli* which it was bound to accept. The union was then formalized by an ordinance of 12 April 1654. Scotland was 'incorporated into . . . one Commonwealth with England', and would send 30 MPs to the new British Parliament created by the Instrument of Government. There was to be free trade between the two nations, and a common system of taxation. Finally, to try and win over Scottish vassals and tenants, all heritable tenures, lordships and jurisdictions were abolished.

This last measure was typical of Cromwell's settlement of Scotland. His aim throughout was to provide incentives for the Scots to co-operate with England. He perceived them less as a conquered people than as godly brethren who had briefly erred but who should now be coaxed back to the paths of righteousness.

It was otherwise in Ireland. Whereas Scotland was treated as a separate kingdom, with a notional right to accept or reject union with England, Ireland was simply assumed to be an English dependency. The design on the Great Seal of England in 1651 illustrates this dramatically. But, though a dependency, Ireland still posed a security threat. In October 1641, the Catholics of Ulster had rebelled and massacred about 3,000 Protestants. Thereafter, the English Parliament was haunted by fear of a Catholic/Royalist invasion from Ireland. Following the Regicide, Charles II initially favoured Ireland as a springboard for an attempt to regain his throne, and in March 1649 Cromwell warned that the Irish would 'in a very short time be able to land forces in England'.

To prevent this, he launched the military campaign which culminated in the massacres of Drogheda (11 September 1649) and Wexford (11 October 1649). He excused these atrocities as divine vengeance for the 1641 rebellion, as 'the righteous judgement of God on these barbarous wretches who have imbrued their hands in so much innocent blood'. Such a belief explains why the Irish settlement was much more punitive than the Scottish.

In January 1650, Cromwell issued a declaration 'for the undeceiving of deluded and seduced people'. He insisted that the English came 'to ask an account of the innocent blood that hath been shed' and 'to break the power of a company of lawless rebels'. This objective became clearly apparent in an Act for the Settlement of Ireland (12

Scone, 1 January 1651: the Scots unilaterally crown Charles II King of Great Britain, France and Ireland. However, his dreams of regaining the English throne were soon to be shattered by Cromwell's victory at Worcester.

August 1652). Having achieved 'a total reducement and settlement of that nation', England set about punishing 'those of higher rank and quality . . . according to their respective demerits'. The rebels of 1641, all Catholic clergy, all those in arms at any stage against the English Parliament, and a long list of named individuals were to be exempted from pardon. Furthermore, all those 'of the popish religion' who had 'not manifested their constant good affection to the interest of the Commonwealth of England' between October 1641 and March 1650 were to 'forfeit one third part of their estates in Ireland to the said Commonwealth'. They were only allowed to enjoy the remaining two-thirds 'in such place' as Parliament appointed. The areas chosen – for security reasons – were Connaught and County Clare. Although Parliament denied any intention 'to extirpate that whole nation', the effect of these measures was to remove at a stroke Ireland's Catholic socio-political élite (see pp. 000–000).

Thus, if Puritan zeal encouraged a gentle approach towards the Presbyterian Scots, it prompted Draconian penalties against Irish Catholics. The Cromwellian union of the British Isles was undoubtedly a bold experiment. For the first time a genuinely British Parliament was created. In practice, however, Cromwell handled Ireland and Scotland in sharply contrasted ways. His rule produced no lasting solution to the problem of a 'multiple kingdom'; and in 1660, sensing that the British Isles were too diverse to be governed by a single Parliament, Charles II abandoned incorporative union.

IX

This brings us to the disintegration of the Protectorate and the restoration of the Stuarts. English political history between September 1658 and May 1660 is extraordinarily complex and a detailed narrative would be inappropriate here. But the outline of events is relatively straightforward, and can be briefly sketched.

I argued earlier that the priorities of Army leaders and civilian politicians remained incompatible throughout the 1650s. While he lived, Oliver Cromwell possessed enough prestige within each camp to allow them to coexist: the republican regimes, though never stable, could at least survive. But Oliver's declared successor, his son Richard, was wholly unsuited to fulfil such a role. Mistrusted by both Army officers and republican politicians, he proved unable to reconcile the inherent contradictions of the Protectorate. As a result, during 1658–60 a series of ill-fated governments succeeded each other with alarming rapidity while the threat of anarchy grew menacingly.

Richard Cromwell inherited an appalling financial position: by the end of 1658, England's annual deficit exceeded £500,000, while Army arrears stood at £890,000. In a desperate bid to improve his revenue, Richard summoned a third Protectorate Parliament for 27 January 1659. Both republican MPs and Army officers disrupted this Parliament, forcing its dissolution on 22 April. The Army then persuaded Richard to recall the Rump Parliament. This in turn refused to recognize the Protectorate, called for Richard's resignation, and re-established the Commonwealth. However, the Army, finding its demands still ignored, expelled the Rump on 13 October and a fortnight later established a Committee of Safety of 23 'to secure the people's liberties as men and Christians, reform the law, provide for a godly preaching ministry, and settle the constitution without a single person or a House of Lords'. This was a last-ditch attempt to enshrine the 'cause' for which the Army had fought; and it rested on the narrowest power-base of any Interregnum regime.

The Army alone had shored up the Republic; now it alone destroyed it. Probably wishing to preserve order, the commander of forces in Scotland, General George Monck, demanded the return of the Rump and marched south. The Committee of Safety, facing mutiny in the North and apprentice riots in London, dispersed on 17 December, and for the next ten days England had no government at all. Chaos reigned until regiments throughout England followed Monck's example and reinstated the Rump on 27 December. When he entered London early in February 1660, Monck secured the re-admission of those MPs 'purged' in December 1648. The restored Long Parliament bowed to the overwhelming public demand for 'free elections' and finally dissolved itself on 16 March. At Monck's suggestion, Charles II issued the Declaration of Breda (4 April 1660) which promised a 'general pardon', 'full satisfaction' of Army arrears, and 'liberty to tender consciences'. It was a masterstroke. The first free elections since 1640 produced the massively pro-Royalist Convention Parliament which met on 25 April and two weeks later passed the momentous declaration of 8 May. The English Republic was at an end.

Although the Restoration Settlement took two years to construct, its basic aim was simple: to turn the clock back to 1641 and to ignore the developments in between. Those statutes to which Charles I had assented remained in force; all others were null and void. England's executive again consisted of the King and Privy Council, its legislature of the King-in-Parliament. The membership, procedure and business of both Houses of Parliament were exactly as before the Civil War. The Church of England was re-established, albeit with narrower doctrine and tougher penalties against dissenters. The years after 1660 also witnessed a marked decentralization of authority to the localities. But these changes pall beside the relentless drive to rebuild old forms of government. All the institutional experiments of the Interregnum were completely obliterated.

X

What, then, had they achieved? Or was it all for nothing? The years 1649–60 still mark an aberration in English constitutional history. To this day, we are governed by a mixed monarchy in which authority is shared between Crown and Parliament. Their nature and powers have changed enormously over the last three centuries, but that has always been achieved by adapting the polity restored in 1660, never by starting afresh. Yet it is precisely this fact which makes the Interregnum so important. Its long-term significance lies not in what it created, but in what it *discredited*.

In his preface, John Morrill likens the Commonwealth and Protectorate to 'a tidal wave' and ensuing floods. In constitutional terms, the most lasting consequence of this was not a subtle change in the eco-system, but the creation of mental 'flood-barriers' to prevent further inundations. The vast majority of those who lived through the 1650s developed a number of strong aversions which subsequently became deeply ingrained within English political culture. In particular, England's rulers became permanently suspicious of paper constitutions; of the use of religious zeal to mould institutions of government; and of standing armies. Most European states have at some time found all these options necessary, even attractive; that England has studiously avoided them since 1660 testifies to the powerful negative impact of the Interregnum.

Let us take each of these themes in turn. England's lack of a written constitution is one of its most distinctive characteristics. Whereas many countries have felt the need for such a document, the experience of the Instrument of Government and *The Humble Petition and Advice* proved deeply disillusioning and engendered a firmly pragmatic approach to constitution-building. As the Marquess of Halifax remarked in the 1680s, 'a constitution cannot make itself; somebody made it, not at once but at several times . . . Its life is prolonged by changing seasonably the several parts of it at several times.' The poet Alexander Pope advanced a similar view in 1733: 'for forms of government let fools contest./Whate'er is best administer'd is best.' This attitude of 'if it works, keep it' is central to English constitutional development, and owes much to the failed experiments of the Interregnum.

But the disillusionment and despair went deeper than that. During the early part of the seventeenth century it had been widely held – by Charles I as much as by Oliver Cromwell – that human souls could be changed by reforming the institutions under which they lived. But, after the Restoration, this belief that religious imperatives should mould forms of government effectively disappeared. Religious 'enthusiasm' was no longer thought a valid guide to constitutional reform. In 1661, Seth Ward, later Bishop of Exeter and of Salisbury, welcomed England's deliverance 'from the tyranny and bloody rage of the wild, fanatical enthusiasts'; while in its 1681 address to Charles II the University of Cambridge insisted that 'no religion . . . can alter or diminish . . . a fundamental hereditary right of succession. Religion became a matter of private faith rather than public duty. That England has not allowed religious zeal to dictate her patterns of government since 1660 is primarily because the Interregnum demonstrated the hazards of such an approach.

Finally, the experiences of the 1650s confirmed and sharpened the

English hatred of rule by the sword. The cry 'No standing armies!' had been heard before 1640, but the episode of the Major-Generals gave it new intensity. As Sir John Trevor argued in January 1657, their effect was to 'prostitute our laws and civil peace to a power that never was set up in any nation without dangerous consequences'. According to another MP, John Stephens, the 'little fingers of Major-Generals [were] . . . heavier than the loins of the greatest tyrant kings that went before'. By the end of the century, John Trenchard was expressing an almost universal assumption when he declared that 'a standing army is inconsistent with a free government, and absolutely destructive to the constitution of the English monarchy.'

Instead, as a bastion against paper constitutions, theocratic states and martial law, the English re-embraced their monarchy. If Charles II's main ambition after 1660 was 'not to go on his travels again', his subjects had equally little desire to embark on further constitutional travels. As Sir Herbert Butterfield wrote, 'from the very experiment of an interregnum, they learned that there was still a subtle utility in kingship and they determined to reconstitute their traditions again, lest they should throw away the good with the bad.' This in turn helps to explain why England – unlike almost every other European nation – did not overthrow her monarchy in 1789, 1848 or 1918. The Commonwealth and Protectorate 'inoculated' England against republican institutions: they persuaded her to restore royal government and if necessary adapt it rather than destroy it. That process of adaptation has changed the monarchy profoundly, but commentators have never been short of reasons for preserving kings and queens – from the Rev. John Whitaker, who stated baldly in 1795 that 'monarchy . . . is the primary, the natural, the divine form of government for man', to Anthony Jay's 1969 aphorism that 'the strength of monarchy does not lie in the power it has, but in the power that it denies to others.' By contrast, apart from brief upsurges during the 1820s and 1870s, England's republican tradition remains the weakest in Europe.

A preference for evolution over revolution, for gradualism over cataclysm: these attitudes are manifest in English political and con-stitutional history since 1660, but should certainly not be attributed to vague notions of 'national character'. Rather, they are responses to particular historical situations, experiences and predicaments. If England's constitutional development displays exceptional continu-ity – at any rate in outward forms – that short, sharp discontinuity of 1649–60 should take much of the praise or blame. To return to John Morrill's metaphor: England's constitutional structures have been extensively modified since 1660; but the dykes built to protect them from another tidal wave still endure.

CHAPTER II

The English Republican Imagination

JONATHAN SCOTT

It was in the realm of ideas that the English Revolution threw down its sternest challenge. An aghast nation had witnessed the execution of a king. It had even proved possible to abolish the monarchy. But how was the *idea* of monarchy to be abolished from the English public mind? There it sat enthroned, not only by all the social and political structures of the time, but by the record of time itself. The Regicide was a declaration of war upon English political history.

Yet it was the very scale of this problem that partly accounts for the subsequent achievement of the English republican imagination. For it was in the same realm, of ideas, that the English Revolution left what may be its most enduring legacy. The slimmer the pedestals of traditional political legitimacy, the greater the imaginative effort required to replace them. From the consequent decade of constitutional instability emerged not only one of the great classics of European political philosophy (Hobbes's *Leviathan*, 1651) but a rich tradition of republican writing including a classic of its own – James Harrington's *Oceana* (1656).

The English republican story begins, then, with the paradox of practical failure and ideological success. The long-term result is a modern monarchical Britain surrounded by states (including the United States and France) partly moulded by English republican ideas. Yet even the practical failure of English republicanism was only complete in the long term. Before its collapse the English Republic had registered some precocious successes. It was by drawing upon these, as well as its broader circumstances, that republican thought contrived, in a life span both troubled and brief, to make an extraordinary intellectual journey.

Within two years of its birth as a sickly infant, every day expecting death, we observe something very like adolescent bravado. This gives way to the reflection appropriate to middle age. Yet in turn this maturity was to spark something more than the natural human desire for self-perpetuation. It is nothing less than a longing for immortality – in Harrington's hands a literal reaching for the stars – that prefigures the republican decline.

I Youth 1649–50

The English people, it has been said, could not have imagined a republican government before 1649. The Republic came into being without the consent of the political nation and against the current of political history. Republican thought was accordingly created by the Republic, not the other way round.

Although there was no native English republican rhetoric, the materials for one were to hand. There was a rich and ancient European republican language. This was in origin classical (both Greek and Roman) and Mediterranean. It was the political culture of the southern city-states, as monarchy was of the north-western territorial kingdoms. Between 1300 and 1600 it had, along with the rest of the classical revival that we call the Renaissance, been recovered and developed by the city-states of the Italian peninsula. From 1500 the Italian became the European (or Northern) renaissance. Throughout the Tudor and Stuart period, England had experienced the influence of a classical and renaissance culture steeped in republicanism, rebellion and war. By the eve of the Civil War both Sir Robert Filmer and Thomas Hobbes had drawn attention to what they considered the pernicious political effects of renaissance literature. Contemporary over-indulgence in Aristotle, Livy, Tacitus and Machiavelli, they said, was doing little to cement the bonds of political allegiance in general, and allegiance to monarchy in particular. By 1642 rebellion and war had come to Britain.

Eventually it was this classical inheritance that would provide the basic language of republicanism in Britain. This resource was identified early by the first and most powerful defender of the Republic, John Milton, who wrote in his *History of Britain*:

> Britain . . . as it is a land fruitful enough of men stout and courageous in war, so it is . . . not over-fertile of men able to govern justly and prudently in peace . . . For the sun, which we want, ripens wits as well as fruits; and as wine and oil are imported to us from abroad, so must ripe understanding and many civil virtues be imported into our minds from foreign writings and examples of best ages: we shall else miscarry.

The full development of this classical republicanism lay, however, in the future. The first task of the Republic was both more urgent, and more difficult. It was to deal with the bitter harvest of 1649: of war, both past and still continuing (in Ireland); of the shocking Regicide; it was to deal with the difficulties of political innovation, both practical and intellectual; with the illegitimacy of a military regime; with a disastrous harvest aggravated by unprecedented taxation. It is hardly surprising that the Republic's first problem was its own deep unpopularity. This difficulty was exacerbated by the populist nature of all republican political rhetoric. In England it was government for the people, over the people, in spite of the people.

Early republican writings are notable, accordingly, for their lim-

---

Key republican texts

John Milton, *The Tenure of Kings and Magistrates* (1649).
John Goodwin, *Right and Might Well Met* (1649).
John Warr, *The Priviledges of the People* (1649).
Marchamont Nedham, *The Case of the Commonwealth of England Stated* (1650).
Mercurius Politicus, 1649–53 (ed. Nedham; these dates describe the period during which the journal was a key republican text. Both it, and Nedham's editorship, continued through the 1650s).
John Milton, *Pro Populo Anglicano Defensio* (*A Defence of the English People*) (1651).
John Hall, *The Grounds and Reasons of Monarchy* (1651).
Henry Vane, *The Retired Man's Meditations* (1655).
Henry Vane, *A Healing Question* (1656).
Marchamont Nedham, *The Excellency of a Free State* (1656).
James Harrington, *Oceana* (1656).
Edward Sexby and Silius Titus, *Killing Noe Murder* (1657).
James Harrington, *The Prerogative of Popular Government* (1658).
Henry Stubbe, *An Essay in Defence of the Good Old Cause* (1659).
Joshua Sprigge, *A Modest Plea for an Equal Commonwealth* (1659).
Marchamont Nedham, *Interest Will Not Lie* (1659).
John Milton, *The Readie and Easie Way to Establish a Free Commonwealth* (1660).
Algernon Sidney, *Court Maxims* (unpublished; written 1665–6).
Slingsby Bethel, *The World's Mistake in Oliver Cromwell* (1668).
Henry Neville, *Plato Redivivus* (1680).
Slingsby Bethel, *The Interest of Princes and States* (2nd edn. 1680).
Algernon Sidney, *Discourses Concerning Government* (written 1680–3; published 1698).

---

ited and defensive nature. Full marks for honesty went to John Goodwin's *Right and Might Well Met* (1649). This defence of Pride's Purge, the Regicide and the Revolution tackled the most difficult problem directly. The public good, explained Goodwin, was not to be confused with the wishes of the public. 'If a people be depraved and corrupt, so as to conferre . . . power . . . upon wicked men, they forfeit their power . . . unto those that are good, though but a few. So that nothing pretended from a non–concurrence of the people with the Army, will hold water.' This was an early statement of what remained the doctrine of leading republicans like Henry Vane junior throughout the Interregnum. The key political objective was 'the public good'. To understand this concept we need to pay more attention to the early modern resonances of the second word than the modern implications of the first. Modern democracies stress the *means*

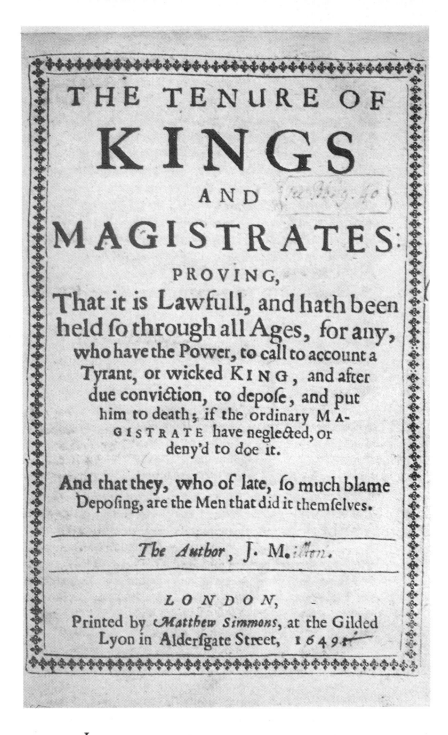

THE TENURE OF KINGS AND MAGISTRATES:

PROVING,

That it is Lawfull, and hath been held so through all Ages, for any, who have the Power, to call to account a Tyrant, or wicked KING, and after due conviction, to depose, and put him to death; if the ordinary MAGISTRATE have neglected, or deny'd to doe it.

And that they, who of late, so much blame Deposing, are the Men that did it themselves.

The Author, J. M.*ilton*.

LONDON,

Printed by *Matthew Simmons*, at the Gilded Lyon in Aldersgate Street, 1649.

John Milton's The Tenure of Kings and Magistrates *published in 1649 was the most famous of all the defenses of the regicide.*

to power: that it be authorized by the people. Accordingly, modern politics has become almost a numerical science. Seventeenth-century republicans were less interested in means than *ends*. The end, 'the public good', was the only legitimation of political action. Politics was a moral science and this end derived its moral value not from the public, who were its *recipients*, but from its author. This was the author of all good: God.

Thus it was as an institution 'unnecessary, burdensome and dangerous to the . . . public interest of the people' that monarchy was abolished by Act of Parliament on 17 March 1649. Thus it was that John Milton, in the most famous defence of the Regicide, *The Tenure of Kings and Magistrates* (1649) explained that magistracy (political power) was authorized by God for the people's good. Magistrates departing from the end of their own institution must be resisted. Conversely 'if all human power to execute . . . the wrath of God upon evil doers . . . be of God; then that power, whether ordinary, or if that faile, extraordinary, so executing the intent of God, is lawful, and not to be resisted.' Marchamont Nedham looked elsewhere to explain the Republic's unpopularity:

> [Machiavelli] compares such as have been educated under a monarchy or tyranny to those beasts which have been caged or cooped up all their lives in a den . . . and if they be let loose, they will return in again because they know not how to value or use their liberty. So strong an impression is made . . . by education and custom from the cradle.

The other thorny problem was innovation. The innovatory nature of the Republic was impossible to hide. There was no more dangerous or formidable accusation in a pre-modern society traditionally navigated by precedent. It is this, rather than the anachronistic concept of democracy, which is the acid test of early modern radicalism. Were the republicans prepared to look political change in the face?

The answer came during what historians have called the Engagement Controversy (1649–51). This followed from the Republic's practical response to its own unpopularity: the requirement that all adult males engage themselves to be faithful to the new regime. One result was '*de facto* theory', which abandoned the high ground of morality altogether. Allegiance to the Republic was demanded on the grounds not that it was good, but that it was a fact. Historians have traditionally (and rightly) emphasized the limited or conservative nature of this theory. But they have not always seen its accompanying radicalism: its grasping of the nettle of change.

'Nature,' wrote Anthony Ascham (*Of the Confusions and Revolutions of Governments*, 1649), 'is in every part sick and distemper'd, and therefore can find rest in no posture . . . all governments carry with them the causes of their Corruption.' Since change was thus inevitable, the important thing became to limit its scope. It was upon these grounds that 'we of the people must be contented with those governours into whose full possessions it is our destiny to fall.' This was hardly a ringing endorsement of change itself, but this recognition of its inevitability (seen as corruption) was the first step along a crucial intellectual road. The second was taken by the remarkable and fearless Nedham.

In Marchamont Nedham's *The Case of the Commonwealth of England Stated* (1650) emphasis remained upon the inevitability of change. '[All] Governments have Their Revolutions and Fatal Periods . . . There is, saith Tacitus . . . a wheeling of all things and a revolution of manners as well as times.' Here change becomes, however, 'generation' as well as 'corruption'. The gloom of Ascham's 'Confusions' has given way to Tacitus's shapely 'wheel'. For underlying this transition is another, of profound importance. From the Christian view, the world is a place of corruption and suffering, a vale of tears; and government is an instrument for the containment of sin. What has replaced it is an older, pre-Christian vision: the classical, and specifically the Greek, in which change is cyclical (rather than linear), and both natural and necessary. If it is the consequence of decay it is no less the precondition of growth. Life entails birth alongside death.

Government must contain sin, but it can also diminish its scope by morally improving (liberating) its people. The culmination of this line of thought came in the work of Algernon Sidney, who served his political and ideological apprenticeship under this regime. Not only are 'Changes . . . unavoidable', wrote Sidney, but

> to affirm otherwise . . . is no less than to . . . render the understanding given to men utterly useless . . . whatever we enjoy, beyond the misery in which our barbarous ancestors lived, is due only to the liberty of correcting what was amiss in their practice, or inventing that which they did not know . . . if it [therefore] be lawful for us, by use of that understanding, to build houses, ships and forts, better than our ancestors . . . to invent printing . . . why have we not the same right in matters of government, upon which all others do most absolutely depend?

Liberty, for Sidney, meant not only liberty from tyranny, but (where appropriate) from history.

None of these early works amounts to much as positive statements of republicanism. In this respect they are limited, defensive. Their objectives are justification and submission. And yet within them is a steely potency which is a portent for the future. In the dark infancy of republicanism, beset by difficulties on all sides, two key ideological boundaries have been crossed. The first is the liberation of a supposedly popular government from the need for public approbation. The second is the early modern intellectual Rubicon, a transition from medieval to modern: an insistence on the right to effect change.

II Triumph (1651–53)

These achievements give us some sense of the power of republican ideology in adversity. What could be expected, should that adversity cease? In the next three years there was a dramatic transition, from defensive to positive argument, from self-justification to republican celebration. This has not always been recognized; nor have the reasons for it. But it followed from one of the most remarkable achievements in seventeenth-century European political history.

Republican writing in this period drew upon certain natural advantages. One was its status as government propaganda, with all of the resources and freedoms that implies. The other was the quality of the writers and thinkers involved, including Milton, Nedham, Sidney, Harrington and Vane. But the development of republican thought between 1651 and 1653 also drew upon the spectacular political accomplishments of the Republic itself. Our view of the Rump Parliament (1649–53) remains negative. It achieved little of note, and nothing lasting. To some extent this reflects contemporary public perception. But it also reflects the political propaganda of the Army, who had to justify its expulsion, for reasons more connected with self than public preservation, in April 1653. What it does not reflect is the republicans' own perception of their experience.

*T*he Great Seal of the Commonwealth (1651) depicted two aspects of the republican ideal: internal liberty ('freedome') as the self-government of a citizen community: external conquest (of Ireland: that of Scotland was in progress).

Lacking political legitimacy, traditional constitutional machinery, or public support, the Commonwealth leaders had to inherit the consequences of a Civil War and Revolution, to face universal European condemnation, and to fight three more wars against its own external enemies, all using a form of political machinery it had itself invented. In the course of this Herculean undertaking, the Rump's leaders discovered not only that government under these circumstances could survive, but that in four short years they had stood the shame of Stuart military weakness on its head. The Civil War and accompanying parliamentary centralization of government had dragged England in one decade through its version of the European military revolution. The Republic was the first English government to inherit this new-found power. By 1653 Ireland and Scotland had been conquered, Charles II had been defeated, the mightiest navy in Europe had been humbled, and Europe's two great powers, Spain and France, were vying for an English alliance. No one involved in this experience ever forgot it, or what it said about the potential for republican (as opposed to royal) power. By 1653 Milton was talking about a 'new Rome in the West'. 'We never bid fairer,' said the MP Thomas Scot, 'for being masters of the whole World.'

It was under the influence of this accomplishment that there emerged what we now know as English classical republicanism. The nation had witnessed the result of government based upon merit, rather than birth. 'When Van Tromp set upon [the English admiral] Blake in Folkestone Bay,' wrote Algernon Sidney,

> the parliament had not above thirteen ships against threescore . . .
> to oppose the best captain in the world . . . But such was the . . .
> wisdom and integrity of those who sat at the helm, and their diligence
> in choosing men for their merit was blessed with such success, that
> in two years our fleets grew to be as famous as our land-armies; the
> reputation and power of our nation rose to a greater height, than when
> we possessed the better half of France . . . [and] all the states, kings,
> and potentates of Europe, most respectfully, not to say submissively,
> sought our friendship.

It was on this European stage that the Republic's case for itself was also put by John Milton. Through the *Pro Populo Anglicano Defensio* (1651) a bemused European public discovered that the Republic was in no mood to apologize for itself. Indeed the absence of monarchy in England appeared to have been supplied by Milton's king-sized ego. His positive argumentation – which spoke from Plato, Aristotle, Cicero and Livy about the beneficial effects of liberty – probably counted for no more than his withering talents for abuse. In Milton's work Claude de Saumaise, one of the foremost political writers in Europe, went down in history as a 'mere grammarian'; a 'boring pedant', 'weevil', 'liar', 'eunuch' and 'rogue'. No more high-profile attacks on the Republic were forthcoming.

The principal credit for laying the basis for English classical republicanism belongs, however, to Marchamont Nedham. The vehicle for

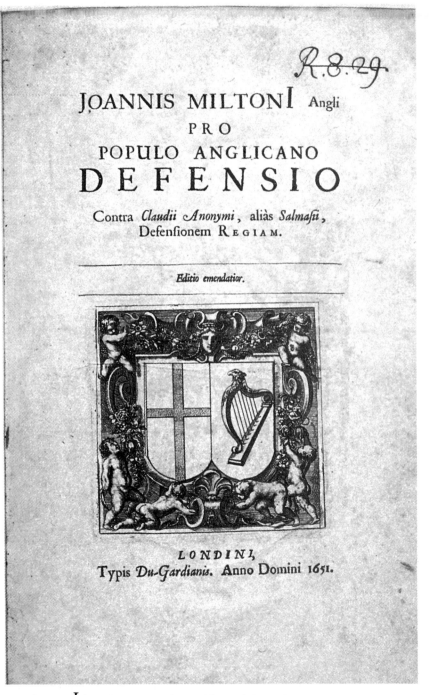

R.8.29.

JOANNIS MILTONI Angli
PRO
POPULO ANGLICANO
DEFENSIO

Contra *Claudii Anonymi*, aliàs *Salmasii*,
Defensionem REGIAM.

Editio emendatior.

LONDINI,
Typis *Du-Gardianis*. Anno Domini 1651.

*J*ohn Milton's latin Defence of the English People *(1651) was a
major vindication of the republic in the face of European condemnation
and the superiority of a commonwealth over a monarchy.*

43

this accomplishment was the Commonwealth's own weekly journal, *Mercurius Politicus*. Under Nedham's editorship this became a lively and highly effective propaganda organ: 'tis incredible', wrote one contemporary, 'what influence [it] had.' This enterprise began in 1649 but it was two years later, under the influence of the Republic's military triumphs, that it began to set forth most clearly its purpose and its theme.

The purpose followed from Nedham's earlier defensive observation, concerning the 'impression . . . made . . . by education and custom from the cradle'. Now with the Republic apparently winning the struggle for its own survival, Nedham's attention turned to an altogether more ambitious objective. This was to change the nature of education and custom in England. Republicanism could not be secure until a new political generation had been raised, educated in the history and the precepts of liberty. The 'greatest error' that could be made in a 'Free State', explained *Mercurius*, was 'keeping the People ignorant of those wayes and meanes that are essentially necessary for the preservation of their Liberty'. It was to supply this defect in the people's education that week by week over three years Nedham issued what amounts to the first ever English classical republican ideology.

Neither the nature nor the principal theme of this ideology will come as any surprise. Nedham drew upon the Greeks, the Romans and the Renaissance Italians to stress the priceless value of political liberty: republican self-government. 'Men have liberty to make use of that Reason and understanding God hath given them . . . to choose their own Governours'. When they did so such magistrates would be chosen for their virtue and merit, not upon the principle of 'Birth and Inheritance . . . [which] must needs be the most irrational and brutish [government] in the world'. Above all, however, Nedham, like Milton, took up that strand of classical republicanism that emphasized the indissoluble link between political liberty and military greatness. This had been considered by Aristotle, had been particularly emphasized by Livy, and had been distilled by Machiavelli. Nedham particularly distinguished himself (from Milton among others) by his open and continual use of the notorious Machiavelli. It was upon the basis of 'the Florentine's subtle discourses upon Livy', interpreted in the light of its own military success, that English republicanism developed its distinctive radical, popular and militaristic character.

The soldier and the citizen, explained Nedham, had to be one. People who made their own laws obeyed them; citizens who governed their own country had the courage, and the incentive, to fight for it. Week by week *Mercurius* rehearsed passages from Livy and Machiavelli drumming home the message that the Romans entered upon the path of greatness as soon as they had overthrown their kings. Everything that was great in Rome 'grew up, flourished, and perished, with her liberty'. 'The same causes will ever have the same effects.' As proof Nedham pointed to 'our own Nation; whose high achievements may match any of the Ancients'. Further exaggerating, Sidney repeated:

> We need no other proof of this, than what we have seen in our own country where, in a few years, good discipline, and a just encouragement given to those who did well, produced more examples of pure, complete, incorruptible and invinceable virtue, than Rome or Greece could ever boast; or if more be wanting, they may easily be found among the Switzers, Hollanders and others; but it is not necessary to light a candle to the sun.

It was thus poised on the brink of world conquest and everlasting fame that the English republicans bumped up against another, and hitherto neglected, fact of Roman history. Rome's liberty, while it may have caused its military greatness, was also destroyed by it. The end came in the form of Caesarian usurpation. On 21 April 1653 Oliver Cromwell dissolved the Rump.

III Hubris

Cataclysmic though it was, this event did not end the development of English republican ideology. Indeed that ideology was poised on the brink of its finest moment. This was the achievement of a man who understood and used the Rump's classical republicanism, but who also transcended it. Alongside Machiavelli he would place the theorist he rightly called 'the greatest [political] writer at this day in the world'. The man was James Harrington, and his *Oceana* (1656) took republican theory where no one had thought it was possible – or wise – to go.

Republican theory had faced the abyss of innovation. It had turned defensiveness to expansionism: to the conquest of space. It now turned, breathtakingly, to the conquest of time. Harrington believed he had found the recipe for political immortality.

This was not something Machiavelli had believed possible. Like the true classicist he was, Machiavelli's response to the political turmoil of his own time had been to embrace it. Change was inevitable: either there would be improvement or decline. The political challenge was to ensure the former. For Harrington, however, there suddenly appeared the possibility of ending political change for ever. Harrington arrived at this position by using intellectual sources unknown to Machiavelli, and alien to Renaissance learning.

Oceana was a challenge to Cromwellian rule. It invited the Protector to legislate himself out of, and Harrington's republic into, existence. And it appeared during a year of more general republican polemic against the rule of a single person. The work is justly famous on three counts.

The first is as the mature and quintessential statement of English classical republican doctrine. Harrington restated the principles recovered by Milton and Nedham. He called this teaching 'ancient prudence' and expanded it into a system. He praised Machiavelli as the 'onely Politician of later ages'; the only recoverer of ancient prudence. Thus it is in *Oceana* that we find the fullest statement of classical republicanism: including the doctrines of the mixed constitution, drawn from Aristotle, Polybius and Machiavelli; the model republics of Sparta, Venice and Rome, also discussed by Machiavelli; of rotation of office; a citizen soldiery; and an equality of property ownership, all discussed by *Mercurius Politicus*.

Oceana is famous, secondly, for its historical theory (also prefigured in a rudimentary way by Nedham). For Harrington's objective was not simply to assert the value of republicanism, but to explain how the English Republic came into being. This reflected his own personal history, for although Harrington had republican friends (most importantly Henry Neville) he had not been a republican himself. On the contrary, he was a close friend of Charles I who 'passionately loved his Majestie' and contracted 'so great a griefe' at his execution that 'never any thing did goe so near to him'. It was accordingly a major function of *Oceana*, as of Hobbes's *Leviathan*, to research the tragedy of the Civil War and to find a way out of it. To this end *Oceana* offered not only an astonishingly detailed political system but, as its basis, an historical analysis of political power.

It was in the course of this analysis that Harrington arrived at his most famous idea: that the nature of a state's political constitution (what he called 'the superstructure') will reflect the balance of its ownership of property ('the foundation'). This 'doctrine of the balance', he declared, 'is as old in nature as herself, [yet as] new in art as my writing'. This use of the language of art and nature – the same language as Hobbes's *Leviathan* – is, as we shall see, a first clue to what Harrington was doing here. The history of property ownership in England therefore explained the history of political power. The English monarchy had perished because in the sixteenth century the balance (predominance) of property ownership in the state had shifted from the nobility to 'the people'. 'Wherefore the dissolution of this government caused the war, not the war the dissolution of this government.' The resulting 'popular balance' could only give rise to a popular (commonwealth) government.

Yet these two aspects of Harrington's work were only building blocks toward his real ambition and (in his view) accomplishment. This was to understand – and eradicate – the causes of political change. This analysis of political history was a preliminary to ending it. For Algernon Sidney, as for most republicans, 'nothing can or ought to be permanent but that which is perfect. And perfection is in God only, not in the things he has created.' For Harrington, however, 'A man is sinful yet the world is perfect, so may the citizens be sinful, and yet the commonwealth be perfect.' If political constitutions reflected the balance of property then in that balance lay the key to political stability. To fix the balance in place would eliminate the causes of political change. *Oceana*'s law for this purpose (one of its 'fundamental laws')

Harrington called the Agrarian. He then erected upon this foundation an extraordinarily elaborate superstructure. More than two-thirds of the work's considerable length is spent rehearsing a series of 'orders' exact down to the last detail. These orders were themselves internally balanced, like a carefully calibrated watch.

The purpose of the superstructure was to guide and shape political participation, which Harrington called 'civic motion'. Every citizen had a role, regulated by rotation. The 'form of the commonwealth', he said, 'is motion'. 'In motion consisteth life . . . [and] the motion of a Commonwealth will never be current unless it be circular.' It was in imitation of the heavens that 'the motions of *Oceana* are spherical'. Order by order 'the people' of *Oceana* were pitched into perpetual circulation, 'the parishes annually pour themselves into hundreds, the hundreds into tribes, the tribes into galaxies.' Thus perfectly organized, the Commonwealth

> should be immortal, seeing the people, being the materials, never dies and the form, which is motion, must without opposition be endless. The bowl which is thrown from your hand, if there be no rub, no impediment, shall never cease; for which cause the glorious luminaries that are the bowls of God were once thrown forever.

This was heady stuff, and we have come a long way here from the language of classical republicanism. The classical tradition was a moral one, opposing the moral qualities of virtue to vice, reason to passion, liberty to tyranny. Despite initial appearances *Oceana* is not, finally, a moral work. It is an outrageous masterpiece of political and historical materialism. Its political analysis hinges upon the material foundation of property. Harrington also refers to his citizenry as 'the materials of the commonwealth'. It was upon fixing the balance of the one, and the motion of the other, that Harrington's bid for political immortality rested. For 'Policy is an art. Art is the observation or imitation of nature.' Nature was the perfect art of God. In *Oceana*, with its endless motion, its wheeling orbs and galaxies, Harrington believed he had actually successfully 'observed and imitated' the universe. By so doing he had harnessed for politics its very immortality. It is difficult to imagine a more extreme political ambition. What Harrington was claiming was to have copied the creation. At the end of *Oceana*, the lawgiver Olphaeus Megelator

> conceived such a delight within him, as God is [said] . . . to have done, when he finished the creation of the world, and saw his orbs move below him. For in the art of man, being the imitation of nature which is the art of God, there is nothing so like the first call of beautiful order out of chaos . . . as the architecture of a well-ordered commonwealth.

What has not been explained here is how Harrington arrived at his understanding of nature. What makes *Oceana* such an extraordinary work is that it fuses together the three greatest intellectual forces of the Interregnum. The first, classical republicanism, provides the means, but it is the second, natural philosophy, which defines Harrington's end. It was Sir Francis Bacon who first identified this objective: the search for the 'pure knowledge of nature', the handiwork of God. The 'true end' of this quest was nothing less than the 'restitution . . . (in great part) of man to the sovereignty and power [over nature] . . . which he had in the First state of creation'. Through this understanding 'natural philosophy proposes to itself, as its noblest work of all, nothing less than the renovation of things corruptible.' From natural philosophy Harrington took both his objective and his method; that is why it is within this tradition that we find the seventeenth-century parallels to *Oceana*'s Utopian form – in Samuel Hartlib's *Macaria* for instance, or Bacon's own *New Atlantis*.

Adapting the Rump's classical republicanism, James Harrington produced the republican masterpiece Oceana *(1656).*

The third major influence on Harrington, however, was Hobbes, and Hobbes's own natural (and political) philosophy. Hobbes's *Leviathan* had been published in 1651, three years before Harrington started writing. On the surface, *Oceana* disputes aggressively with *Leviathan*. But as an astute contemporary noticed: 'though Mr Harrington professes a great Enmity to Mr Hobs in his politiques, underhand notwithstanding he . . . does silently swallow down such Notions as Mr Hobs hath chewed for him.' To this Harrington replied, candidly: 'I have opposed the politics of Mr Hobbes [only] to show him what he taught me . . . Mr Hobbes . . . will in future ages be accounted, the best writer at this day in the world.'

It was Hobbes who first stated Harrington's definition of 'policy' (political science). 'Nature is by the Art of man . . . so imitated, that it can make an Artificial Animal . . . for by Art is created the great *Leviathan* called commonwealth . . . which is but an artificial man.' Hobbes dramatically represented this sword-wielding Super-Man on the cover of his book. Harrington's commonwealth too was a giant man: 'so the parliament is the heart which, consisting of two ventricles, the one greater and replenished with a grosser store, the other less and full of a purer, sucketh in and gusheth forth the life blood of *Oceana* by a perpetual circulation.'

What Harrington borrowed from Hobbes was the basis of his whole system. This was Hobbes's understanding of what nature was. According to Hobbes it was material in motion. This motion would continue perpetually unless arrested by motion, or pressure, from a contrary direction: 'when a thing is in motion, it will eternally be in motion, unless somewhat els stay it.' It was accordingly on the basis of Hobbes's metaphysics, of 'what Mr Hobbes has taught me', that Harrington erected his whole conception of politics, and of the commonwealth. This commonwealth was a republic of 'materials' in perpetual motion. This would 'be immortal, seeing the people, being the materials, never dies, and the form, which is motion, must without opposition be endless'. It was simply a machine, noted one contemporary in disgust, 'like a perpetual motion in the mechanics'.

Not surprisingly Harrington's 'materials' themselves proved sceptical. While his historical analysis impressed, his enthusiasm for converting people into so many wheels and pulleys in perpetuity did not. In so reaching for the stars, Harrington had left the earth. Five years later he had also lost his sanity, imagining himself persecuted by wheeling bees and swooping flies. It was, said John Aubrey, 'the strangest illness I ever saw'.

IV Nemesis

In Greek tragedy *hubris*, overweening ambition, was followed by *nemesis*, retribution. The republican story followed its classical script to the last. *Oceana* was the high-water mark of republican theory. In drawing upon such diverse traditions it greatly enriched subsequent republican debate. The circumstances ushered in by the Lord Protector's death meant that there was such debate in abundance.

Hobbes's *Leviathan* (1651)

Hobbes's *Leviathan* (1651) was the first great work of English political philosophy. It is indeed one of the towering achievements in the history of political thought, and has few equals in the early modern period in Europe. Since it advocated monarchical government, its use by Harrington is on the surface surprising. *Oceana* does, indeed, criticize this and other features of *Leviathan*'s argument. That at a deeper level Harrington nevertheless found Hobbes's teaching irresistible is, however, an entirely understandable tribute to the scale of his achievement.

Leviathan is addressed to the fundamental theme of political obligation. The problem had been posed in no uncertain terms by the recent civil wars. Hobbes rendered it in characteristically extreme terms, stating that, without government, the natural state of man was one of 'war of all against all' with life accordingly 'nasty, brutish and short'. In keeping with this sceptical position, the only universal human impulse Hobbes was prepared to recognize was the selfish desire for self-preservation. It was, since Plato, the problem of converting such individual selfishness into public political and social allegiance that had lain at the centre of European political thought. Hobbes's brilliant achievement in *Leviathan* was to show how the State could – indeed, had to be – constructed from that selfish impulse itself. It was thus erected upon the one secure essential of human political conduct.

Underlying this vision of politics was an equally sweeping view of nature. As part of the created world, man obeyed what Hobbes understood to be the universal laws of nature. Not only a sceptic but a materialist, Hobbes's view of these laws drew upon recent developments in a range of European arts and sciences (*Leviathan* itself was written in Paris). Human life was a war of all against all because nature was nothing but material in perpetual motion (and therefore collision). It was the function of the art of politics to erect an artificial construct of political obligation (the 'commonwealth') in which people bound themselves to one another publicly in order to preserve themselves privately. Despite the desirability of the object (an artificial state of peace, guaranteed by the public sword) it is not surprising that most of Hobbes's contemporaries found this analysis deeply shocking. In a seventeenth-century world where political thought remained a moral 'science' rooted in theology, the infamy of *Leviathan* accompanied and overshadowed its fame.

Cromwell himself had leafed through *Oceana*. Displaying the rugged common sense that accounted in no small part for his own rise to pre-eminence, he declared his refusal to give up power 'won by the sword, for a little paper shot'. This was a materialist analysis of politics of which Harrington could scarcely have disapproved. By late 1658, however, Oliver had been replaced by his son Richard, who had not won anything by the sword. By May 1659 the nation registered the poverty of the practical political imagination by restoring the Rump. There followed a year of constitutional confusion leading inexorably to Restoration of a different kind.

This was accompanied by the richest outpouring of republican theory yet. However, nothing about its quantity could disguise its cause or, increasingly, its tone. The republican experiment was drawing to a close. In this year there were works of 'neo-Harringtonianism' and anti-Harringtonianism – the great majority of tracts registered, in one way or another, the impact of *Oceana*. But there were also restatements of all of the earlier and independent republican languages. These included not only classical republicanism but, for instance, the religious republicanism and language associated with Sir Henry Vane; the interest language associated with the New Model Army; and the continuing republican dabbling in natural philosophy. All this resulted in important works like Henry Stubbe's *An Essay in Defence of the Good Old Cause* (1659); Marchamont Nedham's *Interest Will Not Lie* (1659); and Joshua Sprigge's *A Modest Plea For an Equal Commonwealth Against Monarchy* (1659) which called for 'new and further discoveries into the America of nature'. It is fair to say, however, that the writings of this year were demonstrating the variety and vitality of established republican discourse rather than its capacity for continued development.

The republican experiment perished by the hand of its own creator. It was undone, as it had been begun, by military force. But at a deeper level it fell a victim to the problems of unpopularity, illegitimacy and internal political instability from which it had never been free. That is why for the authentic voice of republican nemesis (and a final blast of invective) we must turn back to that old pioneer, John Milton.

Milton's *The Readie and Easie Way to Establish a Free Commonwealth* (1660) has rightly been criticized for the poverty and implausibility of its constitutional suggestions. But this is perhaps to miss the point. In this tract can be found all the incompetence and incomprehension, the magnificence and wonder, of which the republican experiment was composed. It is a superb, pointless, and entirely uplifting wail of anguish at the destruction of the cause: 'making vain . . . the blood of so many thousand valiant Englishmen, who left us in this libertie, bought with their lives'. For this tragedy Milton blamed, of course, 'the people', rather than himself, or his friends. It was a last act of folly and spite by the 'worthless . . . inconstant, irrational and image-doting rabble . . . not fit for that liberty which they cried out

The last to be consulted. The English people's own verdict on the republic in their near universal welcoming of the Restoration (1660) has stood ever since.

and bellowed for'. Yet concealed beneath this heated language was a serious point. It had been noted by Milton much earlier, in his *History of Britain*: '*Liberty hath a sharp and double edge*, fit only to be handled by just and virtuous men.'

The liberty to choose virtue, *entailed* the liberty to choose vice. The republican experiment fell victim to the very quality by which it had justified its existence. Nedham's attempt to transform popular 'custom and education' in England had failed. External military victory had not been enough to protect the Republic from the enemy within. 'We could never be contented,' explained Sidney, 'till we return'd againe into Egypt, the house of our bondage.' Forced, at last, to make their rhetorical liberty actual the republicans saw its 'sharp and double edge' laid, as they had reason to expect, to the root of the republic itself.

*A*lgernon Sidney, profoundly effected by the republic's military
victories, to which he contributed as a naval administrator, was
later widely influential as a political writer both in Europe
and America.

53

For Sidney this was partly a lapse of memory: 'the people' had forgotten how they had suffered under monarchy. 'Burnt children dread the fire, but we, more childish than children, tho oft scorch'd and burnt, do agen cast ourselves into the fire, like moths and gnats, delighting in the flame that consumes us.' The truth was, of course, that republican dreams, and accomplishments, had to be paid for. The 'English people' had not enjoyed the Interregnum. Upon reflection the 'moths' much preferred the glad, if bumbling, colour of kingship to the black severity of military rule.

Yet did this 'make vain' the whole experience of republicanism in England? The truth is of course that it did not. For if the practice of republicanism had failed to live up to the theory, when the Republic was dead the theory lived on. Even republican practice in England did not expire as a political force, and as a practical political possibility, until the settlement of 1689. After the Restoration there was not only an active republican community in exile but, during the principal crisis of Charles II's reign, a major revival of republican power within the country itself. Between 1680 and 1682 a besieged government found both the City of London and the House of Commons under largely republican control. It was this which ended the crisis by reviving national memories of 1641. The passage to Egypt had to be renegotiated. All of this produced a final revival of republican theory, including Slingsby Bethel's *The Interest of Princes and States* (1680), Henry Neville's *Plato Redivivus* (1680) and Algernon Sidney's *Discourses Concerning Government* (1698; written 1681–3).

Above all the theory lived on. In a short period republican writers had produced a major and distinctive body of English political literature. This had partaken not only of the last phase of the European renaissance, but the first of modern science. It had employed some of the finest literary and intellectual talents in the country's history. And consequently it had done so to face some of the most difficult and important issues in early modern political thought.

Small wonder that over the succeeding two centuries a series of the major thinkers and political actors in both Europe and America acknowledged the English republicans as a decisive inspiration. If republicanism went the way of Icarus – flying too close to the sun, while forgetting that its wings were made of wax – we are still watching the brilliant trail it blazed.

CHAPTER III

The Rule of Law

ALAN CROMARTIE

To seventeenth-century Englishmen politics was a branch of the law. Perhaps their deepest political feeling was a sense of law as a 'bulwark' protecting their property and their personal liberty alike against the 'inundations' of arbitrary power. The law protected them because it was fixed and certain; tyranny robbed their lives of this comforting certainty by forcing them to 'live by one man's will'. Law was, in its entirety, the 'inheritance' of a 'free-born Englishman', and every right guaranteed by law was one of the sacred 'liberties' of the English. Thus no clear distinction was made between rights to life and liberty and trivial pieces of private property. A minor infringement of the latter was the thin end of a wedge that would force open all the defences against popery and absolutism. Popery, of course, was not seen as a religion but as a mask for the limitless avarice of the Catholic clergy, so it was natural to associate the fiscal policies of Charles I with the High Church theology of Archbishop Laud, in a supposed popish conspiracy against liberty and Protestantism alike.

The victors of the civil wars would thus have agreed that Charles I was a 'tyrant', that a tyrant was a ruler who disregarded the law, and that the law consisted in certain 'fundamental' liberties (including all property rights) guaranteed in Magna Carta and elsewhere. The point of setting up a 'free state' was to ensure that the liberties of Englishmen were respected. At this point, unfortunately, their agreement ceased. Everyone believed that there were two sorts of law, 'fundamental' and 'superstructive', but of course there was a wide range of views about the distinction between them. Fundamental law was 'part of the foundations' and therefore older, while superstructive law included everything that had happened since. Fundamental law should not and perhaps could not be changed even by a free Parliament, because the preservation of fundamental rights was not just the product but the very purpose of political institutions. Laud and Strafford had been condemned to death for subverting the fundamental laws; resistance to Charles I had been justified by the spirit of the laws because his popish advisers were trying to defeat the aim of government. These laws were the ultimate focus of loyalty and source of legitimacy, occupying much the same place in seventeenth-century minds that we assign to 'the State'.

In modern Britain law is the tool of a sovereign that stands outside the system created by its will. There is nothing that the

55

Queen in Parliament cannot do, and no way in which one Parliament can bind the hands of its successors. Seventeenth-century Englishmen thought of their legal system rather differently: as something inherently reasonable, created by the application of universally valid principles to the needs of England. Common law was by definition a body of custom whose origins no one could remember, a set of principles which had been observed so long that 'the memory of man runneth not to the contrary'. It drew on the law of nature, the law of God and centuries of experience, and lawyers made extravagant claims for its wisdom.

Sir Edward Coke, the author of the only comprehensive interpretation of common law and its unchallenged 'oracle', described it as the 'perfection of reason', the product of centuries of 'fining and refining by so many learned men', so much so that no mere layman was likely to improve upon it. Magna Carta itself was a 'declaration' of its main points. There was thus no clear distinction between establishing what the law was and what it ought to be: between arguing about law and arguing about politics. This was the source of an uncertainty which arguably made rebellion and radicalism possible. The statement that law was 'the perfection of reason' could be taken conservatively to mean that the pattern of existing institutions could not be improved upon, but it could also be taken radically to mean that existing institutions were illegitimate. Thus the Levellers Lilburne and Wildman were fond of quoting Sir Edward Coke to prove that an Act of Parliament itself might be 'against reason' and therefore void.

A culture without the modern conception of sovereignty faced obvious difficulties in changing its constitution. It is not accidental that the 'constitution' of England (the way the English polity was put together) was synonymous with its 'frame' or 'temperament', and that all three words could be taken as medical metaphors. Kings and parliaments were both capable of distorting the laws, but they could not alter the 'reasonable' response to the country's situation. When the fundamental laws were respected, the country was in a healthy state. Not even the abolition of the monarchy, the Established Church and the House of Lords could alter this fact. Indeed these institutions lost legitimacy only because their existence was ultimately felt to be a threat to the essence of law. The new Republic was from the start at the mercy of the legal profession, because they alone could operate the system on which every government staked its claim to loyalty.

The legal profession, in this context, was a small number of men, educated at the Inns of Court in Holborn, who were judges or advocates just around the corner from Parliament in the central courts at Westminster Hall. The common law, on which they were the ultimate authorities, was an 'unwritten' system, i.e. it consisted in rules and procedures to be found, if anywhere, only in the minds of practitioners. In theory, at least, these principles were customs which had been continuously observed since the coronation of

The Inns of Court

The Inns of Court in Holborn (Gray's Inn, Lincoln's Inn, Inner Temple and Middle Temple) were often described as the country's third university. More than half the original members of the Long Parliament had spent some time there, though many probably used them as convenient boarding houses rather than places of education. Professional lawyers spent seven years there in full-time study, eating together, attending the same church services and taking part in a complicated system of oral exercises. The career of a successful barrister involved rising to the governing body of his Inn (the 'bench'), and giving its members a course of lectures (a 'reading') about some area of the law. The twelve judges and some of the most senior advocates belonged to another institution called Serjeants Inn, where they ate together and established an informal consensus on difficult points. Although the educational side of their activities broke down in the 1640–60 period, these institutions continued to inspire great loyalty in their members. Their existence reinforced the self-confidence and cohesion of the profession by giving the senior lawyers a distinctive way of life.

Richard I, and no other form of law could be allowed except by parliamentary legislation. In practice, early Stuart England contained many flourishing courts which had grown up without parliamentary sanction and followed quite different principles, but nearly all these were abolished when royal power collapsed. In 1649 the common lawyers had a stronger grip than ever before both on legal business and political argument. The legal history of the 1650s is the story of how they held on to their position as the arbiters both of law and of politics.

II Law reform

It may seem surprising that idolization of law was accompanied by hatred of lawyers, but stress on the wisdom of fundamental laws probably bred distrust of the professionals who best understood them. If the essence of law was sound, then the corruption and delay in the court system could only be blamed on the avarice of the individuals who operated it. One difficulty was the perfectly sincere attachment of lawyers to the idea of 'due process'. Fixed procedures which seemed to the layman intolerably clumsy were designed to eliminate the last possibility of error and to make the eventual outcome of cases absolutely conclusive. Professional lawyers prized their system for providing 'certainty the mother of repose', as Sir Edward Coke put it. Lawyers distrusted the Chancery because it was in theory a 'court of conscience' which relieved

*W*estminster Hall, *showing Chancery and King's Bench in session.*
The cramped conditions go some way to explaining the cohesion of the
professional elite.

people against the injustices caused by rigid interpretations of the law; laymen could not see why all courts should not be 'courts of conscience'. Non-lawyers in all cultures are shocked by inefficiency and injustice where professionals see only meticulous and consistent application of the rules.

The greatest difficulty faced by the reformers was their high opinion of the law. The essence of the law, as it existed at some imagined point in the historical past, was the treasured 'inheritance' of the 'freeborn Englishman', but the practice of the courts was clogged with the corruption, delays and unnecessary subtleties introduced by the legal profession. Levellers tended to believe that the existing legal system was an expression of the Norman Yoke, replacing a former state of Saxon Liberty, and that Magna Carta itself was a pale reflection of this ideal. An important symbolic grievance was the role of Norman French as a professional language. The use of the Conqueror's tongue proved, to the minds of many Levellers, all their theories about the Norman Yoke. The use of incomprehensible language, disguised further in the legal records by illegible 'court hand', seemed a classic example of a professional conspiracy against the public. More conservative thinkers thought that all had been well politically as recently as Queen Elizabeth's time, while the practical problems were superficial and could be solved by a few procedural reforms. It was perfectly normal for professional writers to deplore the unwieldy mass of statute law, and call for its rationalization, because statutes were made by particular non-lawyers at some moment in the recorded past; they were younger than the customs of the common law and so by definition 'superstructive'.

The more conservative reformers therefore concentrated on those problems which were endemic to early modern institutions. Offices in the courts were thought of as pieces of property, and their holders were supported through fees payable by litigants. Clerks responsible for writing out documents charged by the page, and naturally cultivated large handwriting so as to maximize their income. Chancery had not yet reached the monstrously inefficient state satirized by Dickens in *Bleak House*, but it was already notorious for the delays in its procedure and the avarice of its officials. Before a litigant even reached the courts he normally had to use a cumbersome procedure involving the sheriff against his antagonist, in which the only sanction was the anachronistic one of outlawry. These and similar abuses, which did not directly affect the interests of barristers, attracted thoughtful criticisms from within the legal profession. Even before the Civil War there had been periodic commissions to investigate the fees in the major courts.

In the circumstances of 1649 it would have been surprising if there had been no further suggestions for legal change. The Republic's more Puritan supporters, encouraged by the extraordinary providences of recent political history, were convinced they lived in a time set apart by God for 'reformation'. Its radical critics used the neglected 'fundamental liberties' as a stick to beat it with. A number of pamphlets united constitutionalism with radicalism by focusing on the unfairness of imprisonment without trial for debt. Debtors' prison, like the unreformed Chancery, survived to be attacked by Dickens. Their basic absurdity was as obvious in the seventeenth century as in the nineteenth. Not all debtors were actually penniless, and many rich spendthrifts led comparatively comfortable lives within the prison walls. It was the genuinely indigent who suffered, because they were confined in squalid conditions on a starvation diet, and prevented from earning money to pay what they owed. Levellers quoted Magna Carta to prove that these institutions were illegal, while noting that they were tolerated by the new regime and that the most famous was run by the notoriously corrupt brother of the Speaker of the House of Commons. An obviously desirable reform could be presented as a return to the 'ancient constitution' and used to paint the Parliament as a tyrant like the former King.

The common element in all the radical literature, including a number of tracts of pure invective, was hatred and distrust of the legal profession. In so far as the more extreme examples offered a justification for their entertainingly abusive language, it was in the belief that lawyers, like doctors and clergymen, were essentially parasitic. They had no obvious productive function in a society that attached great importance to labour in a recognized 'calling'. Interestingly, it was not the richest professionals, the great advocates at Westminster, who attracted the most criticism. The most common complaint, shared by senior barristers and radicals alike, was of the

A typical radical squib. Note the emphasis on the misdeeds of court officials, and the appeal to Magna Charta at the bottom of the page.

swarms of 'beggarly' attorneys, fixers and minor bureaucrats that surrounded the courts. Unlike the barristers they had no established place in the social hierarchy and they could not claim to be the learned repositories of the nation's wisdom. It did not occur to their critics that they were numerous because of demand for their services and 'beggarly' because they were cheap.

In the seventeenth century, like all other centuries, there were many people who wished to change one or another law, but it would be a mistake to group them together in a coherent 'law reform movement' with ideas ahead of their time. There were of course some abuses which attracted the same kind of criticisms they would encounter today. The so-called *peine forte et dure*, the slow pressing to death of defendants who refused to co-operate by 'pleading' (saying 'guilty' or 'not guilty' to the charge), was a barbaric example. Benefit of clergy, which allowed one escape from the gallows to anyone who could read a verse from the Bible, was also attacked both as fundamentally inequitable and as a pointless survival from the Catholic past. But if the early 1650s saw a few attractively humane attacks on the severity and unfairness of criminal justice, it also witnessed a 'moral panic' about the supposed behaviour of extreme sectarians. Some Puritans were outraged at the severity of inflicting capital punishments for thefts of over a shilling, but others were worried about pardons for murder which contravened the biblical principle of blood for blood. The Rump's ordinance imposing the death penalty for adultery was also a 'law reform'.

The most important real common theme was pressure for the decentralization of law and the replacement of useful institutions swept away by the recent triumph of the Westminster courts. The Royalist Hyde was largely responsible for abolishing the courts attached to the Councils of the North and the Marches of Wales, tribunals which might not have been based on common law principles but at least offered a local service. The destruction of the prerogative Court of Requests, which had been a traditional refuge of poor litigants (including a disproportionate number of women) was another dubious benefit of the Revolution. Even more dramatic in its practical consequences was the disappearance of the entire Church court system, based on Roman law, which had handled most litigation about tithes and marriages as well as prosecutions for moral offences like adultery.

Even before these events the English court system had been the most centralized in Europe. The courts in Westminster dealt with cases involving sums of more than forty shillings, a sum which had been made relatively insignificant by inflation. Within those courts business tended to be handled by very few people, because judges had 'favourites', advocates whose clients could rely on jumping the queue for courtroom time. It was not surprising that demands for law reform often boiled down to demands for local justice. An element of almost every scheme was a county land register, through which the ownership of land could be established and recorded without the trouble of going to the London courts. The most important class of grievance, then, was essentially the product of an unplanned situation in which people from Cumberland to Cornwall needed to use the same institutions even for comparatively minor business. Remedying this situation would involve threatening the interests of the community who controlled the central courts.

III The Republic and the courts

Most of the Rump's members had not wanted to kill Charles I, or at least had arranged not to be there at the time, so they had not evolved any constitutional theory to account for, let alone justify, what had happened. They made it illegal to proclaim Charles II King, but it was six weeks before they actually abolished monarchy. An obvious, indeed indispensable, first step was to show their commitment to justice by re-opening the courts. It was noticeable that the MPs sent a delegation to the judges, rather than vice versa. It was also noticeable that their assurance came in two different versions. The judges were told that Parliament would govern by the fundamental laws 'for the good of the people', but the published declaration explained this pledge as referring to the laws 'for and concerning the preservation of the lives, properties and liberties of the people', and reserved the right to do 'what shall be further necessary'.

The gap between the two symbolized the situation of the legal profession. Within the great common law courts the common law rights of Englishmen were rigorously respected. No case was ever directly halted by the government, however embarrassing its implications, and the Leveller John Lilburne twice escaped death because

The trials of John Lilburne

John Lilburne was an unusual political leader, a charismatic radical whose numerous writings consisted largely in accounts of his sufferings at the hands of the authorities. 'Free-born John' appealed from his tormentors to the 'fundamental laws' as he understood them, garnishing many of his arguments with misunderstood quotations from the works of Sir Edward Coke. His greatest exploit was in escaping with his life from two attempts to try him for 'sedition' (a capital charge). The first of these prosecutions was instigated by the Rump in August 1649. His defence was an astonishing display of eloquence allied to sub-legal sophistry, and the presence of a menacingly sympathetic crowd enabled him to dominate proceedings. Lilburne did not reject the court's authority to try him, but he found ingenious objections to almost every element of its procedure. When the foreman of the jury announced his acquittal the resultant shout was heard a mile away. Lilburne's next trial came in August 1653, shortly after the dissolution of the Rump. He had returned without leave from a sentence of banishment and there was no doubt in law that he ought to be hanged. In effect he was daring the government to repeat the earlier fiasco. Cromwell took up the challenge and the trial was widely seen as a personal test of strength between the General and his radical critic. The exiled Royalist Sir Edward Hyde reported confident predictions that the winner 'would hang the other'. Lilburne's defence was centred on the claim that the prosecution had not proved he was the same John Lilburne who had been banished. He was acquitted again, but political reality asserted itself when he was kept in prison and shipped to Jersey. The regime could not afford the humiliation of letting him go. The most amazing feature of the whole episode was the respect for law shown in staging the trial at all.

*J*ohn Lilburne defends himself against a charge of Treason.
A caption runs 'John Lilburne saved by the power of the Lord and the
integrity of his Jury who are judge of law as well as fact, October 26 1649'.
The circle to the right gives the names of the jurors.

of outrageously perverse juries. The lawyers' freedom to operate
their system was ultimately dependent, however, on the existence
of juryless high courts of justice, such as the body which executed
Charles himself, to condemn the regime's Royalist enemies. When
defendants in front of these tribunals objected to this infringement
of their fundamental rights, they were told that they had themselves
consented to it through their parliamentary representatives. Outside
the courts, in fact, the government claimed to be a sovereign,
untrammelled by law; within them it inherited the king's position.

Court proceedings from 1649 to 1653 were held in the name of
the 'Keepers of the Liberties of England', a fictional entity whose title

symbolized the difficulties of the republican government. Their claim to legitimacy depended on their respect for 'liberties' constituted, in the estimation of most Englishmen, by the common law, but these rights included the privileges of the king, the clergy, and the peers. The unpopular tithe system would never have survived the collapse of the Church if the courts had not taken over from the bishops in enforcing the rights of tithe holders. Later in the Interregnum the peers were treated just as they had been in the time of Charles I, while the Protector was regarded as a *de facto* king. Lawyers groping for historical precedents used the example of Queen Elizabeth to prove that the title 'king' was not necessary to royal power.

Even in the republican period, radicals were unhappy about a state of affairs in which nothing had changed except the names on the writs, but they found little support in the Rump Parliament. The lawyer MPs had a justified reputation for co-operation on matters affecting the profession, and the only realistic prospects of reform depended upon military influence. In the autumn of 1650, the Rump did legislate to abolish the use of Latin and Law French and the illegible handwriting of court records. An important symbolic victory for the radicals, its practical effects were very limited. Law French in this period was really just a jargon and the technicalities it conveyed were no more comprehensible when revealed in English. Many lawyers continued to take notes in French for their private purposes, partly out of habit and partly because terminology in a dead language has the advantage of being unaffected by linguistic change. This sop to military opinion was the only reform enacted by the Rump or any other Interregnum Parliament.

By early 1652 the pressure for comprehensive reform was building up again. The Army leadership, led by Oliver Cromwell himself, insisted on the appointment of a Commission composed of non-MPs to investigate the law. The minutes of this body's proceedings show the essential problem faced by the reformers. The investigation into fees and procedures was commendably thorough, and its discussions both practical and detailed. For this very reason, however, its proceedings tended to favour those members with direct practical knowledge. Its first chairman, Matthew Hale, was a moderate Royalist who later claimed that he opposed even useful reforms which tended to create a vested interest in the survival of the Republic. He certainly did his best to prevent the two most far-reaching proposals, for county courts and a county land register. When he lost this battle, he seems to have lost interest in the Commission as well and probably had no hand in the final report. The sticking point was proposals which threatened the coherence of the law and the interests of the leading barristers by removing legal business from Westminster.

The Rump Parliament had acquired the advantage of a workable blueprint, but it showed itself quite unequal to coping with the detail of the law and the filibustering capacity of the lawyers. When he eventually broke up its proceedings, Cromwell complained that

Matthew Hale, Charles II's Chief Justice. Regarded as a Royalist under the Republic; after the Restoration he helped the persecuted nonconformists. Both regimes saw his services as a symbol of their commitment to the law.

it took up three months discussing the single word 'encumbrances' in the Commission's draft. The Nominated Assembly of 1653 disinterred the proposals and began to work through them, but even this body moved painfully slowly. At the time when the cautious party among its members, alarmed at the radicalism of godly colleagues, surrendered power into Cromwell's hands, it had lost patience with piecemeal reform and appointed a committee that was to replace the entire law with a simple written code. Chancery would be abolished outright, and the tithe system was endangered. The dissolution was welcomed by feasts in the Inns of Court.

IV Creeping restoration: the Protectorate and the law

The lawyers gained more than anyone else from the Protectorate. Cromwell's title replaced the Keepers of the Liberties in writs and proclamations, and his apologists pointed out that government 'by a single person' (kingship in all but name) was in accordance with fundamental law. The Instrument of Government of course had no parallel under the old constitution, but the new powers it granted to the executive were to last no further than the Parliament promised for next autumn, and Cromwell was consulting with a number of legal experts about his constitutional position. Two judges notorious for ill-treating Royalists were sacked and Matthew Hale was promoted to the bench.

Cromwell's reward came in the Parliament of 1654, when Hale made a speech supporting government 'by a parliament and a single person'. In April 1655, after the failure of Penruddock's uprising, at least three judges participated in trials in which the rebels were convicted of treason under the common law. Juries were instructed that treason was a crime, not just against the King, but against any Supreme Magistrate, including a Lord Protector. When Oliver died this judgement was cited in Parliament to prove that he had been to all intents and purposes a king, and that Richard was his automatic heir. The Cromwells were rewarded for normalizing the legal situation by being treated as *de facto* (i.e. usurping) kings. Practising lawyers included convinced Cavaliers like Sir Jeffrey Palmer, who had a clerk so bigotedly Royalist that he refused to spell Oliver with a capital O. The common law had long possessed ways of dealing with usurpation and the legal acts of usurpers had always been recognized if they did not affect the legal rights of the true king at his return.

Accepting the king's legal position had, however, the disadvantage that it involved accepting that position's legal limitations. The Instrument of Government, on which Cromwell's power to legislate was based, was a document of no legal status, and the months after the Penruddock decision saw a succession of episodes that effectively did away with it. Penruddock's Rising in the west had been accompanied by an even less successful rising in Yorkshire, and so the assize judges in the North were instructed to try the culprits. Unlike their colleagues, they were told to use the treason ordinance made under the Instrument of Government. They refused and were dismissed by the Protector. Shortly afterwards Cromwell decided to reform Chancery by his own authority, and two of his three senior officials in the court resigned.

Perhaps most embarrassing of all, a merchant called Cony, whose religious and political opinion were almost identical to Cromwell's, sued for damages over customs collected under the Instrument. The government was all too aware that its only defence, a plea of necessity, had an exact precedent. When Charles I was attempting to tax without consent by collecting Ship Money, his lawyers had used the same excuse. Cromwell first tried to stop Cony by throwing his lawyers in prison, but the merchant proved to be quite capable of presenting his simple case without professional help. The Lord Chief Justice of England showed himself sympathetic and either resigned or was sacked. Cony was persuaded or frightened into dropping his case and no one followed his example, but Cromwell was the long-term loser. The vast annual deficit he left his successor was the result of a failure to bite the bullet and impose the taxes Parliament failed to give him. The need to appear a law-abiding common law monarch thus threatened the long-term stability of the regime.

Cromwell's government, like the Rump's, eventually found that it was necessary to use extra-legal means of dealing with its enemies. They took the opportunity of an assassination plot to revive the juryless High Courts of Justice, and so relieved the more conservative judges of their conscientious difficulty in condemning Royalists. Shortly afterwards the assize justices who had refused to try the northern rebels were re-employed. At the same time Cromwell was dealing with a small number of his republican enemies by kidnapping them and immuring them in the Scilly Isles and the Channel Islands, out of the jurisdiction of King's Bench. These tactics, questionable but not strictly illegal, were largely responsible for his later reputation as a lawless tyrant, contemptuous of what he was said to call 'Magna Farta'.

In fact his very illegalities were arguably a product of his respect for legal appearances. Even the High Courts of Justice maintained very impressive standards of procedural fairness. Defendants were treated with scrupulous politeness, two witnesses of a treason were needed for a conviction, and there were even a couple of acquittals. On all these points the republicans compared very favourably with both their predecessors and successors. The High Courts of Justice were necessary because his law officers lacked either the ruthlessness or the competence to pack juries; he imprisoned Cony's lawyers but he did not take the more direct step of halting the case. He thus allowed his options to be limited in return for the legitimacy he evidently felt he needed and which only the courts could provide.

The Protector's implicit deal with the legal profession had its effect on the prospects for law reform, and republicans such as Edmund Ludlow naturally saw the abandonment of such schemes as symptomatic of a wider betrayal. In this they were unfair to Cromwell, who had at least tried, in his dealings with Chancery, to go ahead with his own programme of reform. Later he employed a lawyer named William Sheppard as a sort of one-man Hale Commission. Sheppard was a prolific writer of legal manuals, so his proposals were detailed and well informed, but they showed very little sense of political reality. He proposed to decentralize the system by transferring nearly all judicial responsibilities to an oligarchy of godly JPs. This solution would have run up against the great problem of all seventeenth-century governments: their dependence on the unpaid labour of the gentry. The unpopularity of the experiment with the

Major-Generals showed vividly the political difficulties associated with tampering in the traditional operation of local government. If Sheppard's magistrates were to be godly men, drawn from the Republic's natural supporters, they would be an unrepresentative clique that could be sustained only by military power.

Decentralization presented particular difficulties for an unpopular government, but any effective law reform had to be imposed. Legal change through parliamentary legislation entrusted the cure of obvious abuses to laymen who knew too little and professionals who cared too much about the existing system. In the Parliament of 1656 the legal MPs effortlessly stifled another proposal for a land registry, but the suggestion would probably never have resulted in statute law. The parliamentary discussions of the Hale Commission proposals showed that devising a plausible scheme was only the start of the difficulties involved. The acrimonious Cromwellian parliaments lacked either the time or the political will to make similar efforts, if only because they were too preoccupied with grand constitutional issues for the hard work of detailed reform.

Bitter radicals saw the end of Barebone's Parliament as the result of a conspiracy between Cromwell and the lawyers, and the perceived link between law reform and republican politics was shown by a small flurry of pamphlets when Richard was overthrown. The radicals had a strong case, but they probably underestimated, as

---

From *Every man's case, or lawyers routed* by John Jones (1652)

All men endowed with natural abilities desire two things before they have them, which many when they have them desire to be rid of. That is to say old age and wives . . . In bad men their desire of old age is to prolong their earthly pleasures in their enjoyment of other men's rights, which they possess by force or fraud or both and famishing the right heirs in dungeons while they pamper their own bodies and their imps in sumptuous palaces built upon their prisoners inheritances . . . Bad men desire wanton mercenary wives to be their companions and helpers in mischiefs, as Jezebel was Ahab's, to incarnate and multiply devils as well by their examples of life and conversation as by their natural endowments to accomplish the end of their miscreancy: briefly, to co-operate with them in all endeavours to increase the delusions and dominions of the Devil and the sedition, hatred, and enmity of this world. So that at last they must as brothers in iniquity with Antichrist become possessed of Hell, where there is endless sorrow and gnashing of teeth, a place prepared for them before the world began, from which God deliver us. But are not these also true characters of lawyers?

Cromwell did not, the importance of being seen to uphold the law. One sign which cast doubt on the long-term viability of the last republican regimes was their inability to get on with the legal profession. Matthew Hale retired from the bench at Oliver's death, to be followed by two associates when the restored Rump unwisely reimposed the Engagement as a condition of judicial office. Cromwell had managed, by the end of his reign, to fill the entire bench with its proper complement of twelve judges. By the end of the Michaelmas term in 1659 there was only one judge in King's Bench, and he then resigned his commission on the grounds that there was no one with the constitutional authority to hold a court. Inability either to raise taxes or to sort out legal disagreements was a mark of a system starved of legitimate authority. It was not surprising that the return of the King, the only uncontroversial source of legitimacy, proved the only workable solution.

V Conclusion

The Interregnum left fewer traces in the law than in almost any other area of national life. This seems a surprising outcome if law is thought of as a method of organizing certain social activities, imposed by the will of a sovereign. For seventeenth-century Englishmen, however, it was a way of talking about politics, including the sovereign's rights. Those who accepted its authority, as almost all Englishmen did, were driven to accepting its conclusions about the best, and only proper, way of governing England, a way which included a king, a House of Lords, and a tithe-supported Establishment Church. The result of a compromise with legal values were such unconvincing approximations at monarchy and aristocracy as the Protectorate and the Cromwellian Other House. It was not surprising the English preferred the real thing.

Those who wished to do more than replace the Stuarts with the Cromwells were presented with a tricky dilemma. If they claimed a sovereign power, superior to the fundamental laws, they were flying in the face of generally accepted values, and needed to explain where it came from. There were various theories, but none of them had the persuasive force of an appeal to the 'inherited' liberties of Englishmen, guaranteed by common law. If they made or implied a legal claim to political rights, then they admitted the force of legal arguments, including the arguments in favour of a non-republican constitution. Acceptance of such arguments was the first step on the road to Cromwellian monarchy, if not to a Stuart restoration, and tended to rule out substantial law reform. Regimes which were so uncertain about their legitimacy that they sought above all to obey the fundamental laws were unlikely to challenge successfully the professional custodians of those values. If they worked without lawyers, they would produce ideas of no practical value; if they worked with lawyers they were disadvantaged by fighting on enemy ground. There is still no universal land registry.

CHAPTER IV

The Frustrations of the Godly

ANN HUGHES

In the winter of 1648–9, as they forced through the purge of Parliament and the execution of the King, the Army leaders invited many clergymen for consultation about matters of religion. Forty-seven London Presbyterians indignantly refused: 'We have not forgotten those declared grounds and principles upon which the parliament first took up arms and upon which we were induced to join with them . . . and we trust through God's grace never shall.' The war had not been against the person or royal authority of the King which binding oaths like the Solemn League and Covenant obliged them to uphold. The ministers were contemptuous of the providential and spiritual arguments used by the Army and its supporters: 'The providence of God (which is so often pleaded in justification of your ways) is no safe rule to walk by, especially in such acts as the word of God condemns . . . nor is it safe to be guided by impulses of spirit, or pretended impressions on your hearts . . .'

The Revolution's political character horrified the orthodox godly and threatened to end their hopes of religious reformation. It seemed as if the radical sectaries' impulses of spirit were to be given full rein, permitting an outright attack on a national, comprehensive Church organized on parochial lines and served by an educated ministry maintained by tithes rather than voluntary contributions. Gifted laymen (or, even more terribly, laywomen) claiming an immediate inspiration from God would replace the ordained clergy; literally damnable heresies would flourish while the ignorant and those still wedded to traditional 'superstitions' would be left to their fate. This was not the outcome orthodox Puritans had hoped for when they supported Parliament, often with great enthusiasm, in the early 1640s. Rather, Parliament had been seen as offering the opportunity at last to complete the reformation of the Church begun in the sixteenth century, and the chance of a general godly reformation of society.

Definitions of the orthodox godly inevitably distort a complex, shifting reality. People who were agreed on some issues, notably Calvinist predestinarian theology, might differ over Church government, infant baptism or the limits of liberty of conscience. Broadly, however, the mainstream godly wanted a reformed national Church purged of ritual and ceremony, in which strict Calvinist doctrine was zealously preached by well-educated, well-paid ministers the support of lay authorities. This Church should be an effective institution

Gildas Salvianus ;

The firſt P A R T : *i. e.*

THE
REFORMED
P A S T O R.

Shewing the nature of the Paſtoral work ; Eſpecially in Private Inſtruction and Catechizing.

With an open C O N F E S S I O N of our too open S I N S.

Prepared for a day of Humiliation kept at *Worceſter, Decemb.* 4. 1655. by the Miniſters of that County, who ſubſcribed the Agreement for Catechizing and Perſonal Inſtruction, at their entrance upon that work.

By their unworthy fellow-ſervant
Richard Baxter.
Teacher of the Church at *Kederminſter*.

Luke 12. 47 [Ἐκεῖνος ἢ ὁ δῦλος ὁ γνὲς τὸ θέλημα τῦ κυρίε ἑαυτῷ κỳ μὴ ἑτοιμάσας, μὴ δὲ ποιήσας πρὸς τὸ θέλημα αὐτῦ, δαρήσεται πολλάς]

London, Printed by *Robert White,* for *Nevil Simmons,* Book-ſeller at *Kederminſter.* 1656.

Richard Baxter, frequently seen as the stereotype of an orthodox godly minister, trying to bring about a 'reformation of manners' through careful and regular catechizing of all his parishioners.

of education, discipline and reform, inculcating high standards of religious understanding and moral behaviour through preaching, instruction and, if necessary, punitive action, such as exclusion from the sacrament of Holy Communion. We call many of the clergy who favoured such a programme 'Presbyterians' but both then and now it was a loose term: the Worcestershire godly minister Richard Baxter wrote that people who adhered to 'no sect or party . . . were commonly called Presbyterians by the vulgar'. Unlike their Scottish brethren, few English ministers believed Presbyterianism was the only divinely instituted form of Church government: many had served in an episcopal Church before 1642 and many would do so after 1660. Rather, a Presbyterian government had seemed the best available system in the 1640s, and many of the godly hankered for it in the 1650s. It provided for the co-operation of clergy and lay-men in the parish with ruling elders associated with the minister in examining and disciplining the congregation; and offered a national organization which was based on a series of regional councils and synods rather than on a clerical hierarchy as was the case with episcopacy. 'Presbyterian' is used here for those who preferred a compulsory national Church.

Many leading Independents or Congregationalists, with their close links to the Army, supported the Regicide, and they rejected the binding authority of synods over individual gathered congregations. Independents were also more willing than Presbyterians to concede that there might be situations in which 'gifted' laymen might preach, but most prominent Independents – Philip Nye, Thomas Goodwin, John Owen – were highly educated, ordained ministers whose back-grounds were very similar to the Presbyterians. Men like Nye and Goodwin were poles apart from the uneducated preachers and the radical separatists who rejected a worldly ministry. Although the logic of their position is not always clear to us, respectable Independents were not separatists: their gathered congregations of visible saints who could demonstrate a saving faith and a call from Christ were seen as compatible with some form of non-compulsory national Church. Scores of Independent ministers accepted parochial livings (and the tithes that went with them) trying to serve the general population as well as their gathered churches; many others took the State's main-tenance in other forms. For such men liberty of conscience did not extend to 'papists', 'prelatists' (i.e. unreconcilable Anglicans) or to blasphemers and heretics who challenged orthodox Protestant ideas on issues such as the divinity of Christ or the authority of scripture. Consequently these Independents had at times much in common with the Presbyterians and could be regarded as part of the mainstream 'godly'.

The traditional Protestant aspiration was for a union of laity and clergy, magistracy and ministry, to promote reformation. The godly laity were a minority, perhaps a small minority; a 'godly remnant' in a hostile world, Calvinist elect saints, who confirmed their assurance of

Some terms explained

Classis: the crucial district organization in the Presbyterian system of Church government given legislative form in the 1640s. The ministers and lay elders from neighbouring parishes (9–15 in London, 6 in Lancashire where parishes included several chapelries) met monthly to hear a sermon, settle contentious issues, and supervise parish affairs. The classis was intended by Presbyterians to be a compulsory, comprehensive gathering, but the system had no coercive backing, so attendance was voluntary and parishes were not in fact obliged to accept its decisions. In Lancashire and London the local classes elected representatives to a Provincial Assembly but there is little evidence of this in other areas.

Triers: as they were commonly known, more properly the Commissioners for the Approbation of Public Preachers, were established by ordinance of Oliver Cromwell in March 1654 using the power granted under the Instrument of Government to legislate before the first meeting of Parliament. This was a national body of eminent ministers with a few laymen whose role was to approve new ministers and existing ministers seeking new livings. Its membership reveals the scope of the Cromwellian 'establishment': from reconciled Presbyterians like Stephen Marshall, Anthony Tuckney and Thomas Manton, to the most respectable of the Baptists, John Tombes and Henry Jessey as well as Cromwell's closest associates from the Independents Philip Nye, Thomas Goodwin, John Owen and Peter Sterry. Aspirants for approbation had to supply a testimonial to their capacities from three people, including a minister, and evidence of their valid call to a parish or other official post. (The procedure did not apply to pastors of separate congregations unless they received public money.)

Ejectors: the lay commissioners for the ejection of 'ignorant, scandalous, insufficient or negligent' schoolmasters and ministers, with the ministers appointed to assist them set up on a county basis under the Protector's ordinance of August 1654, confirmed by Act of Parliament in 1656. Although there is evidence for regular meetings of the commissioners in many counties, few ministers seem to have been removed. Most ejections took place in the 1640s.

Act of Uniformity: given royal assent by Charles II in May 1662. All clergymen had to pass three tests or lose their livings: they had to use the revised Book of Common Prayer; renounce the Solemn League and Covenant and any right of armed resistance to monarchy; and be episcopally ordained. Almost 1,000 parish ministers were ejected on 24 August 1662 (St Bartholomew's day) because they could not or would not comply with these provisions.

salvation through ceaseless public activity. The degree to which they were a social as well as a spiritual élite is much debated by historians and the existence of staunchly Calvinist labourers and artisans like the 'tinker' John Bunyan and the London Presbyterian and turner, Nehemiah Wallington, is a qualification against too straightforward an identification of godliness with a comfortable position in the world. But Calvinist Protestantism was a demanding creed, much easier to follow for those who were literate and had the time and the opportunity for both conscientious introspection and the exercise of some public responsibility, at village or county level. There were tensions between godly ministers and the laity: lay, especially parliamentary, suspicion of clerical dominance was a major reason why a fully fledged Presbyterian discipline had not been established by 1649. In general, however, laypeople and ministers both sought discipline and reformation; both feared the religious and social effects of unfettered religious speculation and the radical challenge to the authority of the clergy. They aimed at a godly reformation of manners, at the elimination of vice, and more broadly at the removal of a superstitious culture. They preached and legislated against idleness and immorality, against sports and games especially on the Sabbath, against traditional popish or pagan festivals with their maypoles, feasting and dancing, against the temptations of the alehouse.

This reformation of manners has been seen by many historians as an assault by the educated élite on 'popular' culture, but the godly saw cultural divisions as vertical cleavages affecting all social ranks. Furthermore they identified religious and cultural differences with political ones and so godly reformation had a direct political purpose. Royalism for many Parliamentarians was inextricably connected with vice and superstition: there was an influential stereotype of the hard-drinking cavalier, swearing fearful oaths and leading humbler people astray through the promotion of profane sports and rituals. As Cromwell told Parliament in September 1656 the 'interest' they had opposed, had the 'badge and character of countenancing profaneness, disorder and wickedness in all places'. It was not accidental and not simply an attempt to pass unpopular legislation in a thin house that this same Parliament discussed retaining the Decimation Tax on ex-Royalists on 25 December 1656. As Major-General Lambert complained, Royalists 'are, haply, now merry over their Christmas pies, drinking the king of Scots' health, or your confusion'.

Little positive progress had been made in practice on the reformation of either Church or society in the 1640s. War and its aftermath disrupted local government and gave magistrates enough to do coping with immediate problems. The Westminster Assembly of Divines, entrusted by Parliament with the construction of a replacement for episcopacy, etched out with painful slowness a Presbyterian form of Church government. The hesitations of the laity and the campaign for liberty of conscience by Independents and radical separatists which gained the crucial support of the

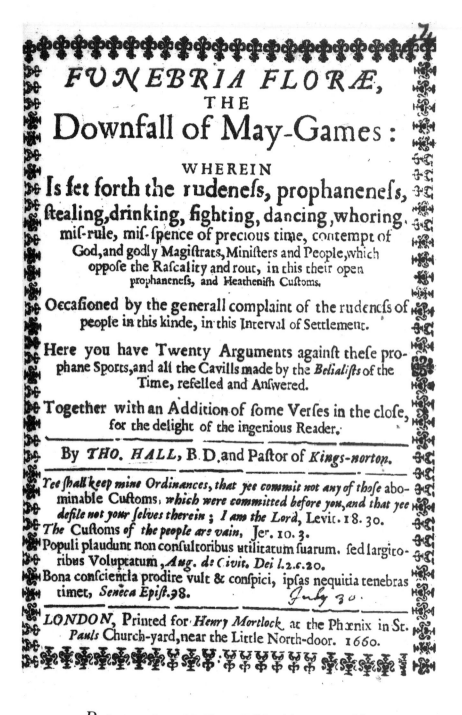

FVNEBRIA FLORÆ,
THE
Downfall of May-Games:

WHEREIN

Is set forth the rudeneſs, prophaneneſs, ſtealing, drinking, fighting, dancing, whoring, miſ-rule, miſ-ſpence of precious time, contempt of God, and godly Magiſtrats, Miniſters and People, which oppoſe the Raſcality and rout, in this their open prophaneneſs, and Heatheniſh Cuſtoms.

Occaſioned by the generall complaint of the rudencſs of people in this kinde, in this Interval of Settlement.

Here you have Twenty Arguments againſt theſe prophane Sports, and all the Cavills made by the *Belialiſts* of the Time, refelled and Anſwered.

Together with an Addition of ſome Verſes in the cloſe, for the delight of the ingenious Reader.

By *THO. HALL*, B.D. and Paſtor of *Kings-norton.*

Yee ſhall keep mine Ordinances, that yee commit not any of thoſe abominable *Cuſtoms, which were committed before you, and that yee defile not your ſelves therein* ; *I am the Lord,* Levit. 18. 30.
The Cuſtoms *of the people are vain,* Jer. 10. 3.
Populi plaudunt non conſultoribus utilitatum ſuarum. ſed largitoribus Voluptatum , *Aug. de Civit. Dei l.2.c.20.*
Bona conſcientia prodire vult & conſpici, ipſas nequitia tenebras timet, *Seneca Epiſt.*98.
July 30.

LONDON, Printed for *Henry Mortlock* at the Phœnix in St. *Pauls* Church-yard, near the Little North-door. 1660.

*P*resbyterian reformers like Thomas Hall feared the restoration of the monarchy was prompting a revival of the 'prophaneness and heathenish customs' of Mayday celebrations.

parliamentary Army meant that the Assembly's programme was only completed in August 1648, shortly before the Revolution of 1648–9 rendered it irrelevant. The Presbyterian legislation was never repealed, but it was never given any official backing after 1649 and in fact the battle for a coercive, comprehensive national Church had been lost in the 1640s. So it is not surprising that orthodox godly were frequently gloomy in the 1650s and that historians have seen them as conservative, embattled failures: 'the 1650s proved not a journey across the Desert to the Promised Land, but a dispirited trek back to Egypt' in John Morrill's eloquent words. But we must be careful of accepting this dark verdict entirely at face value. Godly ministers helped to construct the image of gloom, especially after the Restoration, when they were anxious to present themselves as conservative and so underplayed the advantages they had obtained from Parliament's victory despite the failure to establish an effective state Church.

The godly have rarely been the direct concern of historians who have been more excited by sectaries who took Calvinist ideas to radical conclusions or who rejected them altogether. From a radical perspective, the orthodox godly are élitist conservatives who complicated and mystified religious ideas in order to justify their unjust tithe-taking. More recently other historians have stressed the resilience of 'Anglicanism' with its adherence to comforting Church rituals that matched the natural rhythms of the year, and to the regular worship set down in the Book of Common Prayer which offered hope of salvation to parishioners who led a conventionally good life. From this perspective the orthodox godly are élitist radical reformers who combined an unwarranted interference into the minutiae of their parishioners' lives with the preaching of a complex theology of despair. Ordinary people were required to internalize doctrine which condemned the majority of them to a damnation they could do nothing to avoid.

If we look at the 1650s more directly from the perspective of the godly, the picture becomes more complex; gloom, disillusion and frustration there certainly was, but there were also positive features. Indeed some of the difficulties were seen by the godly as the inevitable consequences of the progress that was being made: 'the devil is still both as crafty and busy as ever, and being now . . . beaten out of his old holds of idolatry, superstition and open profaneness, he is sure to suit his temptations to the times,' wrote one Lancashire Presbyterian in 1655. Those of the godly who were enthusiastic millenarians also combined optimism and pessimism: blasphemies and disorder would characterize the last days, but these were also days of hope, of Christ's return to rule with His Saints. The very fact that there was no realistic possibility of a Presbyterian national Church allowed a process of regrouping and hesitant accommodation among the godly. Men who had fought bitterly over forms of Church government found themselves united in the face of Quaker attacks on the fundamentals of Calvinism, the authority of scripture and any settled ministry. The Cheshire Congregationalist, Samuel Eaton, had engaged in extensive pamphlet polemics with Manchester Presbyterians in the 1640s, but a decade later he sought their advice in dealing with heretical views among his own congregation and Eaton, like many Presbyterians, argued in person and in print against Quakers. With episcopacy removed, and in an atmosphere where there were few limits on views that could be vented in print or in sermons, the zealous Protestant tradition had fragmented in the 1640s and it could never be made whole again. Nevertheless it is important that some divisions occurred between people who had common backgrounds or some common assumptions which made for a more complicated but less polarized religious scene.

Contradictory impulses coexisted within Puritanism: the stress on the individual's consciousness of a saving faith could imply liberty of conscience and separate congregations, but there was an equally powerful tendency towards discipline, reform and building a godly community. This second tendency was found among many supporters of the Regicide, despite the Presbyterian slur that they were driven by undisciplined impulses of the spirit. In the Agreement of the People, presented to the Rump by the Army officers in January 1649, a positive role was envisaged for a national Church in a clause that contrasted sharply with the insistence on the primacy of the individual conscience in Leveller Agreements. The officers wanted the 'public profession in this Nation' (which was not to be popery or prelacy) to be

> reformed to the greatest purity in doctrine, worship and discipline, according to the word of God. The instructing of the people whereunto in a public way (so it be not compulsive) as also the maintaining of able teachers for that end, and for the confutation or discovery of heresy, error, and whatsoever is contrary to sound doctrine, is allowed to be provided for by our representatives; the maintenance of which teachers may be out of a public treasury and we desire not by tithes.

Hence the religious implications of 1648–9 were not nearly as clear-cut as some radicals hoped and many of the orthodox feared. Throughout its existence the Rump was under great radical pressure with petitioners and pamphleteers denouncing the ordained clergy and demanding the abolition of tithes. After the victory at Worcester the millenarian Fifth Monarchists, who believed in the imminence of Christ's Second Coming and His Rule with His Saints, denounced hesitation and delay. The Rump did impose an Engagement of loyalty that many Presbyterian ministers could not in conscience take; many, especially in London and Lancaster, were suspended from their livings and some in these Presbyterian strongholds were implicated in Royalist plots. In September 1650 the Rump passed a Toleration Act that repealed the Elizabethan legislation enjoining attendance at a parish church. It was typical, however, that the Rump's publicity machine was very low key, even shame-faced, about this Act and gave much more prominence to more orthodox measures. For much of the purged Parliament's work was welcome to the godly: a comprehensive survey of the quality and maintenance of the parish ministry was carried out; an act was passed providing additions (or augmentations) to ministers' maintenance out of tithe income confiscated from bishops, from cathedrals and from convicted Royalists; an apparent threat from Ranters and other religious radicals prompted a strict act against blasphemy. Measures against adultery and in favour of proper observation of the sabbath day were the culmination of godly campaigns going back to the later sixteenth century. In 1649 indeed the Rump was within one vote of ratifying the Presbyterian settlement of the 1640s.

A pattern in religious developments was established during the Rump which was to recur throughout the Protectorate. Radical assaults prompted moves for unity among the more orthodox with a spate of pamphlets stressing the common ground between Presbyterians and Independents and attempts by groups of leading ministers to establish agreement on 'fundamentals' of doctrine and Church government. In 1652 the leading Independent John Owen put forward proposals for the approval and removal of ministers, and for agreement on doctrine; from the Presbyterian wing, Richard Baxter was also busy mobilizing support for a preaching ministry. Similar moves to find agreement were made in the 1654 Parliament in response to alarm aroused by the views of John Biddle (who was accused of denying the divinity of Christ) and in 1656 as a result of the even greater fears provoked by the Quakers. The accession of Richard Cromwell prompted further discussions. Agreement was never reached: the widespread urge to find common ground and to reject meaningless and divisive forms inspired negotiation, but once discussion was under way men too often rediscovered their own particular sticking points. Policy over admission to the sacrament of Holy Communion was one divisive issue. On the other hand, some feared that fundamentals might be defined too restrictively and outlaw valid beliefs. In the 1656 Parliament, most members supported harsh punishment for the Quaker James Naylor, whose entry into Bristol they saw as a blasphemous impersonation of Christ's entry into Jerusalem. Others were more cautious: as Lord Strickland said, 'we know how laws against Papists were turned upon the honestest men. We may all, in after ages, be called Quakers.' None of the godly believed in religious toleration as some absolute good and all worried that liberty might lapse into a licence that allowed heretical beliefs. But faced with practical restrictions many Independents and Baptists gave priority to liberty of conscience.

The failure to establish agreement on fundamentals was a serious set-back, but the ultimate failure of such moves is not the only point. The existence of a continuing dialogue between men who felt they had a common purpose in preserving the purity of religion, propagating the gospel and defeating heresy is an equally important

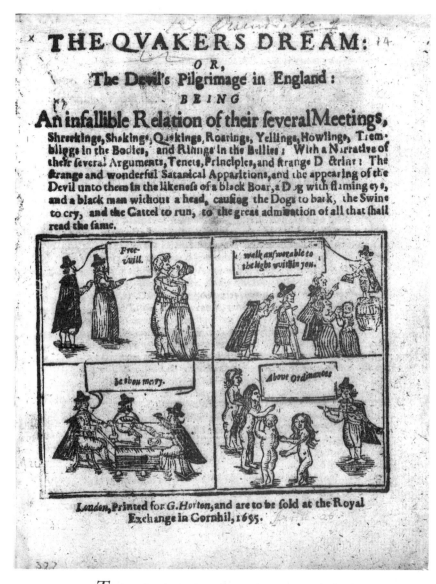

THE QVAKERS DREAM:

OR,

The Devil's Pilgrimage in England:

BEING

An infallible Relation of their several Meetings, Shreekings, Shakings, Quakings, Roarings, Yellings, Howlings, Tremblings in the Bodies, and Rlungs in the Bellies: With a Narrative of their several Arguments, Tenets, Principles, and strange Doctrine: The strange and wonderful Satanical Apparitions, and the appearing of the Devil unto them in the likeness of a black Boar, a Dog with flaming eys, and a black man without a head, causing the Dogs to bark, the Swine to cry, and the Cattel to run, to the great admiration of all that shall read the same.

> Free-will.
> walk answerable to the light within you.
> be thou merry.
> Above Ordinances

London, Printed for G. Horton, and are to be sold at the Royal Exchange in Cornhil, 1655.

To the godly, the Quakers represented not puritan radicalism but a lack of self-restraint, a willingness to indulge in the pleasures of the flesh which they then claimed to be a following of an inner call.

aspect of the experience of the godly in the 1650s. A clear expression of differing attitudes is found in the contrasting behaviour of two groups who both held Calvinist beliefs and both practised adult baptism. 'Open communion' Baptists were willing to work with other independent churches who did not practise adult baptism; their leaders were part of the 'Cromwellian establishment', serving as

Triers and engaged in broad debate on fundamentals. Other Baptists, though, were strict separatists who held that adult baptism was an essential part of a true Church; they were obsessed with following the minute detail of the scriptures and with preserving their own congregations from the taint of the world. They organized themselves into associations that policed individual congregations and lovingly preserved their identity and integrity, but at the cost of abandoning the outgoing preaching endeavours that had gained them support in the 1640s.

If orthodox aims were not fulfilled, the hopes of radicals were comprehensively dashed. When the Barebone's Parliament attacked tithes and lay patronage, its more moderate members quickly resigned their power. By 1656 Cromwell was insisting, 'I should think I were very treacherous if I should take away tithes, till I see the Legislative power to settle maintenance to them another way.' The fundamental parochial organization of the Church was preserved; under the Protectorate a start was made in rendering it more effective by amalgamating tiny parishes and dividing large ones using the 1650 survey as a guide. Cromwell himself clearly represented the twin drives for liberty and reformation; in a series of ordinances passed before the meeting of his first Parliament he rationalized the procedures for awarding augmentations of stipends to preachers out of state funds; sought to purge unsatisfactory ministers; and brought some order to the system of ordination and appointment of ministers through the establishment of the 'Triers'. Except in the case of convicted Royalists, lay patronage rights were respected. Wholesale transformation of the Church was thus ruled out and lay patrons were one of the main protectors of 'Anglican' practices, but most of the godly at least welcomed the relative stability of the mid-1650s. In 1656 Cromwell lauded the Triers as 'such an Approbation as never passed in England before', and Richard Baxter gave their work an equally favourable verdict. Problems of morale indicated by vacant parishes persisted in many areas, however: nine of the fifteen parishes of the second London classis lacked a minister in 1648 and twelve of these parishes had no settled ministry throughout the 1650s.

If we move from an examination of general policy to the experiences of ministers in the provinces, we find many positive features. Many godly clerics were busier and more prosperous than ever before, with greatly expanded opportunities to preach at lectures, regular exercises and meetings, public fasts and the like. 'I now enjoyed great liberty to work and had work enough to do,' wrote Adam Martindale after the Restoration,

> preaching twice every Lord's day to a great congregation . . . preaching of many funerals and baptizings, besides no few occasional sermons at the chapels in the parish. I had my part also, in maintaining one [preaching] exercise in Staffordshire yearly, two in Lancashire and four in Cheshire, besides the great running one of many speakers in those eastern parts and the lecture in Chester.

The expanding book trade, and contacts between London and the provinces developed during the Westminster Assembly enabled obscure ministers to publish their sermons and pastoral works to an unprecedented extent. Tithes were often resented, by radical and Anglican parishioners alike, but many parish ministers seem to have been prospering. Several had their incomes augmented by the State. From 1654, when the system was tightened up, some £1,000 a year was paid to about thirty Warwickshire ministers (one-seventh of the total). The range of those willing to take public money reveals something of the nature of the Cromwellian establishment: in Lancashire and Cheshire it included the Baptist John Wigan and the Congregationalist Samuel Eaton, as well as most of the prominent Presbyterians like John Angier of Denton and Richard Hollingworth of Manchester. An unlooked-for but positive byproduct of religious freedom was that it became possible for the orthodox godly to concentrate on a spiritual élite of intimates in their parish. They could ignore the less godly to an extent that was not possible before the Civil War.

Few godly ministers were in fact prepared to abandon the ungodly, however, and the resistance of many of their parishioners to their discipline and their teachings was a perpetual frustration. There were bitter conflicts over strict admission to the sacrament – by ticket only after stringent examination in many parishes. The veteran Puritan Thomas Gataker complained that many of his parishioners withheld their tithes, 'because I admit not all promiscuously to the Lords table'. A young man refused admission to the sacrament by Adam Martindale because his wife had been pregnant on marriage went off and joined the Quakers. His 'offence', clear-cut to a godly minister, was not seen as such by many parishioners. In perhaps a third of parishes, the communion was suspended altogether for fear of the conflicts caused by restriction (but the surviving records are patchy, and difficult to interpret). In most areas, 'promiscuous' (i.e. open) 'Anglican' practices survived. Examples abound even in Presbyterian heartlands. When the Presbyterian minister of Oldham, Lancashire, was suspended in 1651 for refusing the Engagement, his place was taken by John Lake (later one of the seven bishops of the Church of England who defied James II in 1688). He would only examine strangers and young people before the sacrament, admitting the generality of adult parishioners. There was nothing the Manchester classis could do to stop him. In London, throughout the 1650s, the Royalist diarist John Evelyn could take communion according to the old Book of Common Prayer at the Easter and Christmas festivals denounced as pagan by the authorities. Harassment was only intermittent.

The godly's ambitions and expectations of their parishioners were higher than ever before, which only increased their frustration at the gap between aspiration and reality. Attempts to bridge the gap foundered on the unreasonable demands made by the godly. The

A godly élite defend themselves against the 'poison' of the times

Adam Martindale, from whose post-Restoration autobiography this passage is taken, was born in Lancashire in 1623 and served as a clerk in Parliament's Army. Encouraged by the godly, he became a school-teacher and then a minister, first in Manchester and then from 1649 in Rosthorne, Chester. He was ordained by ministers of the London Presbyterian classis, fearing the examinations required by the Manchester classis were too stringent for a young man who had not been to university. Martindale was deprived of Rosthorne in 1662 under the Act of Uniformity; thereafter he lived by teaching mathematics and as a private chaplain to the Booths of Dunham Massey, preaching publicly when he could.

About the beginning of the year 1653 the opinions that were rampant in the army infected also the country, and some belonging to the Church of Duckinfield (so called) were thought to be deeply tainted. Mr Eaton [pastor of the Independent congregation at Duckinfield], thinking to search the sore to the bottom, propounded a good large number of questions for his people to answer; which were brought into my parish when I was sick. The people that were most eminent for profession of religion, being enured to keep up work-day conferences, began to consider of them, and had gone through the first question, concerning the doctrine of the Trinity, before I was able to keep them company; but at the second (which was concerning the divinity of Christ and the Holy Spirit) I came in to their help. And our way was this: every one that was able brought in his answer in writing, to which, if anything considerable was added by word of mouth, it was noted down at the meeting. Then the papers were delivered to me, to draw up all that was pertinent into one, adding what I thought further useful. This being finished, the number of copies desired was very great, and of writers that could copy them out truly so small, and (considering withall that this little thing might probably be useful to many in other parts) we thought best to print it, and published it was, with my preface and name to it, and this is the true history of the birth of that little Axiomaticall Catechism called An Antidote against the Poyson of the Times.

Lancashire Provincial Assembly, like other bodies, made repeated attempts to revive the general practice of catechizing or instructing of parishioners through a process of question and answer – 'the long neglect thereof is sadly lamented'. But the Manchester minister Henry Newcome described intermittent and unsuccessful catechizing drives in his town, while Adam Martindale complained that in a vast parish like his, 'multitudes of the people would be dead . . . ere we would go once over them'. Most of the 'old ignoramuses' managed in any case to be out when he called. Worcestershire ministers complained that, 'we find by sad experience that the people understand not our public preaching', while in Cumberland and Westmorland ministers resolved, in examining parishioners for admission to the sacrament, not to 'expect from the ordinary sort of people (who through want of breeding, and other natural defects, are usually unable well to express their minds) a distinct or continued discourse of these things, and therefore we shall be satisfied if we can but perceive that they understand the substance.' They would 'take care not to make a question more difficult by our dark and cloudy expressions: but must endeavour to propound things in the plainest terms we can'. Many of these good intentions were contradicted by another resolution of the Cumbrian ministers, not to rely on rote learning: they would avoid on purpose the 'words and method of ordinary catechisms' to ensure their flock had internalized the godly message.

The ignorant and profane (in the judgement of the godly) were probably the most numerous among their parishioners, but it was the open and dramatic assaults by the radicals that were often most unsettling to godly ministers. Baptists and other Calvinist separatists became increasingly defensive and inward-looking, as already suggested, but the Quakers roamed aggressively over most of England with a strong base in many rural areas, whereas earlier sectaries had been concentrated in towns, particularly garrisons. Quakers were often unpopular with all ranks of the local community, regarded as violent, strange outsiders. But their vivid message that men and women should embrace the light within, thereby achieving immediate union with Christ, was attractive to many impatient and disillusioned with the Calvinist stress on the inescapability of sin and the details of the scriptures. Quakers were a public scourge of godly ministers whom they denounced as hypocrites and hirelings, preaching 'by the hourglass' for unjust wages. Quakers heckled ministers in church and street, 'pelted' them with denunciatory pamphlets, pasted accusatory queries to church doors and challenged them to debate.

The assaults by the Quakers were the most direct threat faced by godly ministers at a local level, but they did at least encourage moves towards greater grass-roots co-operation among the godly. The failure to establish a coercive Presbyterian system made Church activity on a broader than parish level very difficult. In Lancashire and London where Presbyterianism had 'formidable strength', that contradiction in terms, a voluntary Presbyterian system, survived to the Restoration. The shortcomings even in these successful areas vividly highlight the lack of general Church organization. In London eight of the twelve planned classes operated in practice, to some extent at least, but the organization was heavily dependent on the enthusiasm of ministers and leading laypeople. In Manchester, also, the classis

Weake as you say we are, yett wee command
all flesh to fall, that doth against us stand.
The light within us, of such force is found,
showld satan come, twill lay him on the grund.

The Light they talke of keepes a heavy rout,
ile search all corners, but ile find it out
By yea and nay, she is a dareing Gule,
ile ly a fall or els I am a Churle.

With face of brass, this woman that you see
most Impudently doth afirm, that shee:
The mind of God, in all poynts, more doth know,
then from the Sacred Scriptures, ere could flow.
Presumptious wretch; it were more fitt that shee,
at home showld keepe, and mind hir howsewifery.
And if noe meanes to live on, worke for bread,
then idlye gossop with hir maget head.
Their light within doth so prevayle.
it makes them hot about the tayle.
Exsept afraind that poynt doth cleare,
they could them selves in pecces teare.

*The Quakers claimed to be guided by the Holy Spirit, but their
enemies saw them as being guided by the Devil. Note the
accompanying verse: 'Impudently doth affirm that she/The Mind
of God in all points doth know/than from the sacred scriptures ere
could flow.'*

An Essex Minister and the Quakers

Ralph Josselin was minister of Earls Colne, Essex, from 1641 until his death in 1683. He served as chaplain to the Essex county forces in 1645 and was very close to the Parliamentarian lord of the manor of Earls Colne, Richard Harlakenden. Good fortune and the protection of local notables prevented Josselin's ejection at the Restoration although he was harassed by the ecclesiastical authorities for not conforming to the ceremonies of the restored Church. These extracts are from the voluminous diary he kept throughout his life.

3 July 1655: preached at Gaines Colne, the Quakers' nest, but no disturbance, God hath raised up my heart not to fear, but willing to bear, and to make opposition to their ways in defence of truth . . .

28 July 1655: the Quakers set up a paper on the church door at Earls Colne. Lord, I and people and truths are thine, I pray thee take care of them . . .

11 April 1656: heard this morning that James Parnell, the father of the Quakers in these parts, having undertaken to fast forty days and nights, was die. 10 [10 April] in the morning found dead . . . the Lord awaken those thereby, that give heed to the light of their own spirits, and will not put themselves under the direction of word and spirit; thus God chooseth the delusions of sinners . . .

31 August 1656: . . . Robert Abbot senior in the street told Thomas Harvey, there cometh your deluder. Lord we are a contempt and scorn, look upon it, oh Lord, and heal it . . .

8 September 1656: employed at Mr Pelham's . . . Quakers there who pitifully scorn the ministers. One said as I and Mr Nicholls went in, woe to the false prophet, I thank God their bitterness puts no provocation on my spirit against them . . .

31 October 1656: In the lane set upon by one called a Quaker, the Lord was with my heart that I was not dismayed, I had some discourse with him, the Lord be my help, I see my own emptiness daily on all occasions.

was powerless to influence parishes that did not wish to heed it, as the activities of Lake in Oldham illustrate. In the absence of coercive authority, the Manchester classis became a voluntary gathering where like-minded men heard a sermon, discussed common problems and examined and ordained young ministers. Attendance depended on the minister's wishes: vain attempts were made by Manchester to secure the participation of the chapelry of Chorlton in the late 1640s, but an enthusiastic minister arrived in 1658 and thereafter Chorlton men regularly attended the classis.

In the other six counties, where some real effort was made to establish Presbyterianism, success was even more limited; in many areas ministers accepted that a coercive system was impossible and turned instead to voluntary associations, pioneered by Richard Baxter in Worcestershire. These associations sought to bypass contentious issues of Church government and provide support for godly ministers in their struggles against both the radicals and the easy-going opponents of their reforming attempts. They were established in a variety of ways in some seventeen counties, but even in Worcestershire the association only included about a third of the county's ministers. For participants they did provide collegiate ministerial activity without the supervision of a bishop or the State. By the later years of the Protectorate, orthodox godly ministers including many Presbyterians had moved far from the alienated position of 1649–50 and had a prominent place in such Church organization as existed. The range of men who served as Triers (see page 00) was parallelled locally by the spectrum who accepted public money, provided testimonials to the Triers, and served as assistants to the ejectors: in Lancashire and Cheshire Presbyterians like Charles Herle, Richard Hollingworth, Henry Newcome, and Isaac Ambrose, joined Independents like Eaton and Michael Briscoe.

No comprehensive reforming and disciplinarian state Church was achieved in the 1650s: overall godly aspirations were clearly frustrated. In more limited and qualified terms, however, the decade was not without its advantages in enabling the godly to preach with official encouragement to those who would listen to them. The godly had not yet acknowledged the failure of their project of transforming Church and society and indeed would not come to terms with it before the end of the century. In the 1650s they were far from being defensive victims and they kept on trying – reviving again and again projects for instruction of the reluctant; and unceasingly defending orthodox views in print and in public debate against radical sectaries, especially the Quakers. So throughout the 1650s the godly can be found in optimistic as well as pessimistic mood; they were baffled but not defeated. Nehemiah Wallington gave up his devotional writings in despair in 1654; in the same year Thomas Gataker's will bemoaned the 'iniquity and distraction of the times'. But Simeon Ashe, preaching Gataker's funeral sermon, praised the 'threescore Presbyterian ministers' in London 'who preach profitably and live godly' and three years later Edward Reynolds compared London to Jerusalem as 'a city of truth, a holy mountain . . . in regard of the doctrine of truth and holiness preached therein'. In Lancashire in 1659, John Angier looked back on the 1650s as including many years of plenty for 'heavenly manna'.

If we look briefly at godly reform in general we find an equally patchy picture. The Puritan programme for moral and cultural transformation went back to Elizabethan times and in counties like Essex the peak period for attacks on bridal pregnancy, alehouses and other objects of reforming zeal was already past. In some areas, like Lancashire, the 1650s was a period of godly advance, but in most parts of England reformers faced the same old difficulties. Everyone opposed wickedness, but not everyone agreed on how to define it.

We have already seen how Martindale's opposition to pre-marital pregnancy was divisive: most villagers deplored the economic and social disruption brought by bastardy, but bridal pregnancy caused no practical problems. Local opinion was not impressed when a determined campaign against alehouses by Robert Beake, the mayor of Coventry, merely increased the number of ex-alehouse keepers dependent on the poor rate. John Pickering, a north Yorkshire JP from a minor gentry and military background, was an indefatigable seeker-out of swearers and met frequently with incomprehension and resentment, especially from his social superiors: one man fined ten shillings for saying 'by mass' immediately followed it up with a 'so God help me' – which he claimed was not an oath 'but a vehement affirming'.

All central authorities of the 1650s encouraged godly reform, at least at the level of rhetoric, but, when so many local people saw it as a self-defeating and unnecessary prying into people's lives, it required very close routine co-operation by all local officials to bring rhetoric and reality together. The Interregnum governments were too preoccupied by other matters, and too lacking in general support to secure this co-operation. The Major-Generals, appointed in the aftermath of Royalist conspiracies, were intended to stimulate local governors and 'encourage and promote godliness and virtue, and discourage and discountenance all profaneness and ungodliness'; as suggested above, their moral and their security functions were seen as part of the same project. Some, very energetic, Major-Generals succeeded temporarily in invigorating local government: Charles Worsley in Lancashire literally killed himself in his determined campaign against alehouses. But the Major-Generals were often inexperienced, had too wide an area to cover and were in effective service for only a matter of months. Cromwell's claim in September 1656 that they were 'more effectual towards the discountenancing of vice and settling religion, than anything done these fifty years' is not supported by local evidence. Even in well-governed Puritan Coventry, where Beake worked closely with Major-General Whalley, godly ministers tried to limit Beake's fanatical sabbatarianism, and the alehouses were reopened almost as quickly as Beake closed them. It seems that moral reform moved to a rhythm independent of much national political change: the 1600s, 1650s and 1690s all witnessed peaks of reforming zeal, but in some areas, like Yorkshire, there were more alehouse prosecutions in the 1660s than in the 1640s and 1650s. The removal of the Church courts during the Interregnum may indeed have removed a vital means of achieving local discipline without putting anything effective in its place.

The limited but real advances and successes achieved by the godly in the 1650s evaporated in 1659–62. The political upheaval of 1659 reopened many of the fissures of 1649: in the Manchester area Booth's rising sabotaged an emerging agreement between Independent and Presbyterian leaders and brought a temporary breach

*T*o the radicals, the 'priestcraft' practised by Presbyterians
was as false and as harmful as that practised by the Roman
Catholic Church and the disbanded episcopal
Church of England.

between Samuel Eaton and his Presbyterian friends like Martindale
and Newcome. The vast majority of the orthodox godly, the 'Presbyterians', welcomed the return of monarchy, but many at the same
time were in despair at several aspects of the Restoration. There was
a real fear of the revival of pagan and idolatrous practices; at the
level of central policy (if that is not too grand a term) there was a
sharp change from a support for godly reform to an encouragement
of 'traditional' culture. The cliché that maypoles came back with
Charles II is supported by evidence from all over England. For the
Worcestershire Presbyterian, Thomas Hall, 1660 was a 'good time

to die'. For many godly ministers the Restoration had a disastrous impact on their careers and social functions. The unfolding calamity is poignantly revealed in the diary of Henry Newcome of Manchester who moved rapidly from being a member of a professional élite to unemployed depression. In the summer of 1660, Newcome went on a sentimental journey back to Cambridge; as the son and brother of clergymen he had contacts everywhere. He dined with masters of colleges; in Derby, Peterborough and other towns he was entertained by prominent ministers and laypeople and usually invited to preach. On his return to Manchester, however, Newcome found that a rival claimant had been preferred to his living – 700 other godly ministers were displaced in 1660 because an ejected Royalist cleric or someone else had a better claim. Newcome continued to preach as deputy to his supplanter until the Act of Uniformity silenced him altogether along with many other godly ministers. On Sunday mornings he recorded sadly, 'I was somewhat afflicted when the time came that I use to go up to my study to prepare for the public and now had not that work to do.'

The Restoration reveals the limits of godly endeavour during the 1650s. After 1660 it was impossible to re-establish a national Church that would include all English Protestants. Liberty of conscience had allowed radical separatists, such as Baptists and Quakers, to develop the organizational and personal strength and identity that enabled them to survive a period of persecution and take advantage of the limited religious toleration permitted after 1689. The orthodox godly were in a more traumatic position for the whole thrust of their activities in the 1640s and 1650s was to combat separatism and they took a long time to understand that they would never again be a prominent part of a national Church. Ministers in the Manchester area (including Angier who like Josselin neither conformed nor was ejected) 'discoursed about the point of separation and all to a man to avoid that are resolved to be present and to join in the service'. The line between a necessary nonconformity to Church practices they opposed and an illegitimate separatism became harder to maintain as the prospect of changing the restored episcopal Church receded and as the ejected clergy themselves continued to minister illegally to congregations of the godly. Many indeed took advantage of Charles II's Declaration of Indulgence in 1672 and were licensed as ministers of Presbyterian congregations – a tacit acknowledgement that they were now a distinct sect rather than an unrecognized part of a national Church. Presbyterians had done enough in the 1650s to ensure that a significant minority of their flock (like Martindale's group) would stand by them in the dark years, protecting them from intermittent Anglican persecution and joining them in worship when possible. Slowly and reluctantly many of the orthodox godly built the distinct networks, academies and chapels that made up the dissenting or nonconformist tradition influential especially in towns and among middling social groups. They were helped by Charles II's own desire to secure some protection for those outside the Anglican Church and by the fact that at times Anglicans themselves, alarmed by the rise of popery, were very reluctant to harass respectable Nonconformists. The late seventeenth century thus saw the halting emergence of the split between Anglican Church and dissenting chapel – a fissure which has had a profound influence on English political, cultural and educational life until the twentieth century.

The boundaries between Anglican and Dissenter were frequently blurred, however – partly because most 'Presbyterians' maintained some contact with the national Church throughout the Restoration period, but also because not all of the godly left the Church. Ralph Josselin in Essex and John Angier in Lancashire are typical of many who did not conform to the required ceremonies, but who escaped ejection through official bungling, powerful protectors or simple obscurity. The 1650s thus secured the 'Low Church' tradition within Anglicanism – scripturally based, Calvinist, committed to lively preaching and energetically anti-ritualistic.

The godly in the 1650s had not sought to build 'dissent', non-conformity or a Low Church tradition; they were not aiming for a world where social and moral reform was promoted by consci-entious individuals or by voluntary societies; they did not intend to develop or protect a distinctive, introverted middle-class or urban culture. With all these they have been credited by historians, but the godly themselves would not recognize them as achievements. They had worked for a general reformation of Church and society, a reformation that would transform the religious understanding and moral behaviour of the whole population. Their partial success only underlined the over all failure of the godly.

CHAPTER V

The Impact on Society

JOHN MORRILL

I

Revolutions have frequently seen massive and irreversible transfers of wealth and power from one social group to another. This is most obviously true of the socialist revolutions of the twentieth century such as those in Russia, China or Cuba. But it is true of other and earlier revolutions such as the 1789 revolution in France, which effected the permanent transfer of property rights to the small peasant away from the noble landowner. The consequences of that transfer are still visible today, and still felt today, as the European Community's Common Agricultural Policy demonstrates.

The English Revolution is different. Or rather it is different in the narrow sense. The Civil War and its subsequent political revolution threatened to bring with it a massive transfer of social wealth and power; but that threat was never realized. What *might* have happened, however, can be seen by looking first at what *did* happen in Charles I's other kingdoms. There, the English attempted, and in the case of Ireland achieved, a social revolution comparable with those mentioned above.

II

By the later 1640s Ireland was a seventeenth-century Lebanon. Catholics were fighting one another as well as the Protestants; pro-Royalist Protestant settlers were fighting pro-Parliamentarian Protestant settlers and both were fighting the Catholics; and everyone was fighting the Scots. The violence and slaughter of those wars was out of all proportion to that on mainland Britain. By the time Oliver Cromwell, adopting Irish rules of engagement, had completed his astonishing military subjugation of the island, two separate forces were working for a fundamental redistribution of wealth and power in Ireland: state indebtedness and a thirst after vengeance.

In order to pay for its earlier campaigns in Ireland, the Long Parliament had raised loans on the security of 2.5 million acres (1 million hectares) of Irish rebel lands. By 1652, more than 1,000 Englishmen held claims as 'Irish Adventurers'. In order to pay for its later campaigns, Parliament had paid its troops partly in cash and partly on the promise of Irish estates. By 1652 some 30,000 soldiers had such claims. Here was reason enough for a vindictive settlement. But Cromwell had no doubt that in Ireland he was fighting an enemy

By the Commissioners appointed for Stateing the Arreares of the Souldiery (and of Publique faith Debts in Ireland)

UPon Composition and Agreement made with *Mrs Ellin Hunt Administratrix to her late Husband Capt Thomas Hunt Deceased in behalfe of her selfe and for the use of Henry Thomas Beniamin Anne, Hester and Sarah Hunt Children of the said Defunct* for all the said Defunts ——— Arrears for Service in *Ireland* from the *Last Day of December 1646 to the 5th Day of June 1649 As Capt of a troope of Horse in Coll Chidley Cootes Regiment*

£ 78 8
714. 17. 06

There remains due from the Common-wealth to the *said Ellin Hunt and the said Children of the defunct their* Executors, Administrators, or Assign's, the Sum of *Seaven hundred and flowerteene Pounds Seaventeene Shillings and Six pence* —— which is to be satisfied to the said *Ellin Hunt and said Children of the Defunct their* Executors, Administrators, or Assign's, out of the Rebels Lands, Houses, Tenements and Hereditaments in *Ireland*; or other Lands, Houses, Tenements and Hereditaments there, in the dispose of the *Common-wealth* of ENGLAND. Signed and Sealed at DUBLIN the *Sixe and twentieth* day of *May* 1658

Examined and entred

Tho Herbert
Iohn Taylor

Edw Roberts
Iohnt Gorges
Rob Geoffreys

An example of a "debenture", a certificate given to every soldier stating his arrears of pay and exchangeable only for Crown lands in England or (as here) land confiscated from Catholics in Ireland.

incapable of receiving and obeying the Word of God. In a meeting with the Irish at Clonmacnoise, he said that he had come to 'extirpate popery'. In its Act of Settlement the Rump spoke of dealing with the Irish 'according to their respective demerits'.

These two motives intertwined to cause the triumphant English to confiscate all the land of all Irish Catholics who could not prove their unstinting loyalty to the English Parliament (some task!) and to herd those Catholics into Connaught (the area between the Shannon and the ocean) where those entitled to hold land could do so, although even there a strip one mile (one and a half kilometres) wide along the whole of the coast was reserved for the government.

The process proved beyond the administrative capacity of the government, and the Adventurers, desperate to find tenants to work the farms and so pay rents, prevented the mass removal of Catholics from the land itself. But huge areas were handed over to more than 600 Protestant Adventurers (largely absentee landowners) and to some 12,000 English soldiers, most of whom stayed on at the Restoration. Although some original owners were able to do a deal with Charles II and get partial restoration in the 1660s, the pattern of landowning in Ireland was transformed. The share of Irish land owned by Catholics dropped from three-quarters to one-fifth. A new landowning class of different ethnic, religious and cultural origins was imposed by brute force. Ireland underwent a revolution in 1649 when its monarch was beheaded.

III

In Scotland, the great landowners had a desperate time in the 1640s and 1650s. But the outcome was different. The nobility, who had led the Scottish Revolt of 1638–41 ('the National Covenant'), were divided about the good sense of joining 'the Solemn League and Covenant' with the English Parliament against the King in 1643–7, and had disintegrated in the face of the events of 1648–9. One group had fought for Charles in the second Civil War ('the Engagers'); and their estates were forfeited by their Scottish enemies after their defeat. But the Covenanters then divided into those who supported Charles II as King after the execution of his father and those who did not (but who still opposed the 'ungodly' English who had deserted the Covenant). In this confusing situation, most of the Scottish élite were sentenced by someone else to lose their estates, and indeed many Scottish peers were expropriated and some were even to die begging in the streets (Charles I's Scottish Lord Treasurer, the Earl of Traquair, is the most spectacular, but not the only, example). At least half the nobility had lost most of their estates by 1660. The English did not add many new confiscations after their military conquest and occupation. Instead they sought systematically to destroy the social basis of the power of the whole Scottish nobility. Cromwellian legislation gave security of tenure on low rents and fines to all tenants (something many English peasants sought in vain), abolished all feudal dues, and above all

*T*he Cromwellian land settlement in Ireland. The figures give (for
each county) the percentage of land confiscated (1653-65) from those
in possession in 1641.

abolished every aspect of the 'seigneurial regime' by which lords
had run provincial Scotland. Gone were the hereditary sheriffdoms
and the heritable jurisdictions of the great Lords; in were itinerant
judges, English soldier-/Scottish laird-shared sherriffdoms and local
courts baron manned by freed peasants.

It was all very deliberate: Colonel John Jones wrote in 1653 that
'it is in the interest of the Commonwealth of England to break the
interest of the great men of Scotland, and to settle the interest of the
common people upon a different foot from the interests of their lords
and masters.' By 1658, Cromwell was claiming success. He told his

last Parliament that no longer did the great Lords of Scotland make their tenants 'work for their livings no better than the peasants of France'. Rather the meaner sort had had 'plentiful encouragement' and the middling sort were purring contentedly.

It was not to last. It was the nobility who were restored in Scotland in 1660, rather more than it was the King. And it was a nobility restored with no restraining hand present to prevent them making good their losses at the expense of the meaner sort.

An essential lesson for the social historian is this: the Regicide unleashed a revolution in landownership in Ireland and a briefly successful revolution in social relations in Scotland. In England it unleashed a lot of anxiety, but not much more.

IV

For many pamphleteers the overthrow of monarchy was seen as a prelude to the overthrow of the social order of which the king was the apex. Landlords had upheld the King's authority, said the True Levellers of Buckinghamshire, and in return he 'doth defend, uphold, maintain and allow them to rend, tear, devour, rob, spoil, extort and tyrannize over the poor people and to this end doth invest them with strange names and titles . . . as dukes, princes, earls, marquesses, viscounts, lords, barons, sirs, esquires, gentlemen'. The putting down of the Lords 'will be the restitution of our rights again'. Indeed, members of the Rump Parliament initially seemed to have some sympathy with this view. Only a week after the execution of the King, on the first occasion when the mini-Rump of the House of Lords first disagreed with the Commons, the Upper House was swept away as 'useless and dangerous'. The peers were not stripped of their titles, but they were stripped of their distinctive legal privileges. They were to play virtually no formal part in the high politics of the 1650s: no more than seven peers sat in any of the parliaments of the Interregnum; and the abolition of the Lord-Lieutenancy removed the office from which the peerage had dominated local government. But, *informally*, the peerage remained quietly influential. They continued to be accorded precedence in any local social event – leading the mourners in funeral processions and so on. They continued to exercise very considerable authority as patrons of the clergy and (albeit in a muted way) in parliamentary elections. Most of the peers spent the decade quietly restoring their financial position. A recent, very detailed, study concluded that by a sophisticated playing of the mortgage market and by finding ways of sheltering behind legal protections, most were able to make significant progress back to prosperity by 1660. The peerage were ready and able to reclaim their dominance of English political life from the moment of the Restoration.

The abolition of the Lords a week after the execution of the monarch was the nearest England came to a social revolution. By the time the Protectorate came in, concepts of nobility were back in

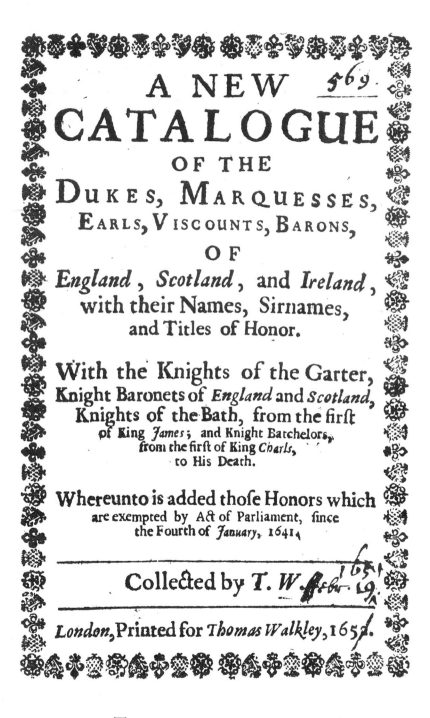

A NEW *569*

CATALOGUE

OF THE

DUKES, MARQUESSES, EARLS, VISCOUNTS, BARONS,

OF

England, *Scotland*, and *Ireland*, with their Names, Sirnames, and Titles of Honor.

With the Knights of the Garter, Knight Baronets of *England* and *Scotland*, Knights of the Bath, from the firſt of King *James*; and Knight Batchelors, from the firſt of King *Charls*, to His Death.

Whereunto is added thoſe Honors which are exempted by Act of Parliament, ſince the Fourth of *January*, 1641.

Collected by *T. W.* *febr. 19.* *1651*

London, Printed for *Thomas Walkley*, 1652.

The abolition of the House of Lords did not diminish public interest in the peerage and catalogues such as this continued to appear.

favour. The Lord Protector had no doubt that he could and should ennoble his closest allies, and that he could dub knights. In 1659, Richard Cromwell sent out the heralds on a national visitation to record and confirm coats of arms. In 1657 a second chamber was added to the Parliament, which many of those close to the Protector were happy to call a new House of Lords, to be formed principally by a new peerage, but including hand-picked representatives of the old one.

Although some radicals called for the outright abolition of peerage titles, and although many pamphlets called for justice against oppressive landlords, hardly anyone demanded the abolition of private property or the levelling of men's estates. The Levellers consistently denied that this was their aim: rather they sought the restoration of enclosed land to the common people, greater equity in the law of property, the abolition of servile tenures and the conversion of copyhold tenures into freehold. Defending themselves against the charge that they were social Levellers in 1649, Lilburne, Overton and Walwyn wrote that 'for distinction of Orders and Dignities, we think them . . . never intended for the nourishment of ambition, or subjugation of the People but only to preserve the due respect and obedience of the people which is necessary for the better execution of the laws.' The Quaker George Fox used language as opprobrious and bitter as any: 'some are in plenty, destroying through superfluity; others being in poverty, which are ready to perish through want of the creatures, raise up thoughts in them to steal.' But his remedy was the conversion of the rich, and their recognition of a duty of charity: 'them that are rich might take away the occasion, and prevent temptation, or take them into some employment.' Even the Diggers, who did indeed see the institution of private property as part of the Fall of Mankind, and who sought to take over commons and wastes and establish on them communities based on common ownership, consistently claimed that they did not intend to expropriate the rich: 'we shall not strive with sword and spear but with spade and plough . . . Freedom gotten by the sword is an established bondage to some part or other of the creation.' The rich must be persuaded by example to surrender their superfluity of property.

These circumstances help to explain why there were so few *social* implications in the treatment of the defeated Royalist party. Anyone with goods worth £200 or more and who could be shown (to the satisfaction of a quasi-legal local tribunal) to have voluntarily assisted the Royalist cause in any of the civil wars of 1642–51 was liable to have his (or, in the case of widows, her) estates confiscated ('sequestrated') and administered by the State. Some 4,000 people were affected, including 94 of the 136 peers, between one-quarter and one-third of all knights, and perhaps one in six of all esquires and gentlemen. Most of these (the major exception was those Catholics who had borne arms) were allowed to pay fines and to be restored to their estates. These 'composition' fines varied in size, but most

The Diggers

On 1 April 1649, just two months after the Regicide, Gerrard Winstanley, a failed merchant tailor and religious visionary, William Everard, a cashiered New Model soldier, and about thirty others took over a barren hillside in Surrey and set up a commune there to grow and to live off vegetables. Later in the year they moved to uncultivated common in the nearby parish of Cobham, where they planted 11 acres (4 hectares) of wheat and built six or seven cottages. The next spring they sent out emissaries who appear to have persuaded small groups to set up similar experiments in seven other counties. The Council of State had ordered the Army to suppress them at the outset, but Fairfax had sought compromise. However, relentless sabotage by local farmers and prosecution before Quarter Sessions brought the Cobham experiment – and probably all the others – to an end by the summer of 1650. The inspiration came from Winstanley's visions (especially one where he pronounced *Worke together, Eat bread together*), the essence of which is captured in this extract from *The True Levellers' Standard Advanced*, a pamphlet of 20 April 1649:

> *And the first reason is this, that we may work in righteousness and lay the foundation of making the earth a common treasury for all, both rich and poor, that everyone that is born in the land may be fed by the earth his mother . . . all looking upon each other as equals in the creation; so that our maker may be glorified in the work of his own hands, and that everyone may see he . . . loves his whole creation and hates nothing but the serpent, which is covetousness branching forth into selfish imagination, pride, envy, hypocrisy, uncleanness . . . For it is shewed to us that so long as we or other doth own the earth to be the peculiar interest of lords and landlords, and not common to others as well as them, we own the curse that holds the creation under bondage.*

represented less than two years' income, and were thus a burden comparable with providing a dowry for an extra daughter. About 800 gentry refused to negotiate with what they saw as an illegitimate regime, or were forbidden to enter into composition. Their estates (a majority of which lay in the six northernmost counties of England) were sold on the open market. However, detailed work by several scholars has revealed that most of their land was purchased by agents acting on behalf of the sequestered Royalists. Three-quarters of all the land of the 61 Yorkshire families and three-quarters of all the land lost by 106 Lancashire families in the Acts of Sale was recovered by the original owners. Although land worth well over £1 million was put on sale, the total amount reaching new owners was probably worth not much more than £20,000 a year, that is, rather less than the holdings of each of the six wealthiest peers. Even if a similar amount of land was sold by ex-Royalists to meet their war debts and to raise composition fines, it is clear that few great families were financially ruined as a result of the civil wars. Indeed, Gordon Blackwood, the historian of Lancashire who has undertaken the most thorough of all studies of seventeenth-century landownership, concluded that 'the Great Rebellion saw neither the enrichment nor the impoverishment of the old, nor the emergence of a new parliamentarian gentry. Nor did it see the emergence of a new royalist gentry.'

If there was no massive expropriation of the defeated party, was there a major infusion of new blood into the ranks of the great landowners? Between 1646 and 1654, successive regimes sold off most of the former Crown lands, and the estates belonging to the bishops and to the cathedrals. These altogether constituted a further £4 million worth of sales. The records are difficult to interpret because so much land was initially purchased by men who then passed it on to others, and records of such secondary transactions are hard to find. But it seems that as far as Church lands were concerned, the main beneficiaries were principally families already well established in the middling and lower reaches of the gentry, who took the opportunity (as they had taken every opportunity over the previous hundred years) to consolidate their holdings. It would also seem that most purchasers were local men, or, so far as the many London-based purchasers are concerned, frequently men born and brought up near where they now acquired estates.

The only significant new group of landowners was created by the sale of Crown lands. For the Rump decided to restrict the purchase of these to holders of military 'debentures', certificates of arrears given to all serving and former soldiers. These could be and were sold by the soldiers for cash and at a discount (often for only half their value) and many senior officers amassed large amounts of credit which they used to acquire substantial estates: six officers acquired lands valued at more than £10,000, and twenty-seven more acquired land worth at least £5,000. But again most of these officers were from gentry backgrounds (the largest purchasers included Lambert and Fleetwood). The number of *nouveaux riches* non-gentle landowners – men like the former drayman Thomas Pride who acquired Queen Elizabeth's favourite haunt at Nonsuch Park in Surrey, or the former candle-maker John Okey who became a substantial landowner in central Bedfordshire – is less than a quarter of the top 50 purchasers.

V

Proscription of convicted Royalists from public office, together with the determination of many neutrals and disaffected Parliamentarians not to associate themselves with usurpers, certainly brought about significant changes in the personnel of local government. A majority of the JPs during the 1650s came from families that had not sat on the bench before 1642. Most local studies have confirmed that the

*J*ohn Okey, *one of the New Model officers who profited most from the wars and acquired a large estate made up of former royal properties.*

proportion from middling and lower gentry families is much higher. But what we are seeing is not so much a shift of power *from* the gentry as a shift *within* the gentry. Indeed, the power of special militia commissioners, of assessors for the monthly assessment (property taxes) and of the 'ejectors' (who regulated the parish clergy), all drawn from the same gentry families as the JPs, may actually have increased local gentry power. And this shift becomes less marked after 1649 as alienated families reconsidered their decision to boycott the illegal regimes, especially when the Lord Protector lured them back with his policy of 'healing and settling'.

It seems likely that the effect of the changes was less dramatic than during James II's attempts to woo Dissenters by his massive purges of local government (to remove all hard-line Anglicans) in 1687–8. Similarly, those who exercised real power at the centre (those on councils of state or headed government departments) came largely from established gentry backgrounds or had successful mercantile or legal careers behind them. The pen-pushers and petty bureaucrats came from significantly lower social backgrounds than their predecessors under the early Stuarts; but they had little real power.

There was, then, no major redistribution of social power as a result of the Regicide. The social structure, and the distribution of wealth within that social structure, differed little from any point in the preceding period. The long-term consequences were minimal. A study of the Restoration JPs concluded that more than 95 per cent who were on the quorum in the 1670s and 1680s were themselves the sons of peers, knights or esquires.

VI

The Civil War had a traumatizing effect on many working farmers and those who lived and worked in the countryside. In the early years of the Interregnum, the main property tax was bringing in £120,000 per month. In the 1620s a grant of five subsidies worth £300,000 over several years was widely held to be insupportable. Although the social spread of assessment was wider and caught both the gentry and the smaller farmers more effectively, it was a crushing burden, especially conjoined with the excise (the forerunner of VAT) on main household goods and especially on salt (essential for preserving fish and meat) and beer (this was the age before tea, coffee or drinking water, and the average consumption of all adults may have been six pints — about three and a half litres — of 'small', i.e. weak, beer a day. The wretched harvests of 1647 and 1648, possibly the worst of the century, sent prices to record heights despite heavy government intervention (see information box 2). High prices would help the larger grain farmer, but not that majority of households who had to buy in stocks of grain. A study of Norfolk has suggested that one result of this crisis was permanently to change and to enhance the levels to which local authorities were willing to subsidize the poor. But despite widespread calls for the reform of the Poor Law legislation and some local experiments, especially in London, both the structure of poverty and the strategies for alleviating distress remained largely unchanged (and were to do so until well into the nineteenth century).

Most contemporaries remained fatalistic about the existence of poverty, seeing it as an unavoidable part of the human condition and as a challenge to the charitable instincts and responsibilities of the rich. But the pamphlets of the period also reveal a body of thinking that started from a sharper social critique. Poverty could be attributed

Agricultural prices in the English Revolution

This table gives the price of agricultural products for each year in the mid-seventeenth century. They are corrected against the overall average for the years 1640–1750. Notice the exceptional high grain prices for 1647–9, by far the highest for the whole period (only three other years in the whole period saw grain prices above 140 — 1661, 1698 and 1709.

(Source *The Agrarian History of England and Wales*, vol. V.ii, *1640–1750*, ed. J. Thirsk (Cambridge, 1985), p.847.

Harvest year	Grains	Other field crops	Livestock	Animal products	Average – all agri-cultural products
1640	104	100	71	95	93
1641	100	92	67	129	97
1642	105	104	70	101	95
1643	92	88	75	94	87
1644	88	91	90	95	91
1645	97	77	94	95	91
1646	132	94	89	112	107
1647	173	115	98	117	126
1648	166	122	101	117	127
1649	164	123	99	135	130
1650	121	95	111	137	116
1651	118	115	88	110	108
1652	109	97	78	100	96
1653	72	103	100	98	93
1654	60	89	98	84	83
1655	97	107	90	84	95
1656	114	135	87	90	107
1657	116	95	85	102	100
1658	123	112	93	107	109
1659	126	96	97	108	107
1660	110	87	101	112	103

to the greed of the landowners and the inequities of primogeniture and enclosure. But the remedies proposed were almost always not the expropriation of the rich so much as the instruction of them into the religious duty, economic prudence and political necessity of discharging their responsibilities more fully.

VII

Successive regimes in the 1650s were at least as firm as pre-war governments in upholding the rights of those who enclosed and engrossed common and waste land and against the poor who lost out. The early seventeenth century had seen a slackening of enclosure in the Midlands plain, the site of the worst disturbances in the sixteenth century, but prolonged and relentless activity in the ancient woodland regions of the West and in the fenlands of eastern England. No regime challenged the right of the lord of the manor to make business deals with contractors and speculators to clear scrub or drain fens and to divide the reclaimed land with them, nor the right of those who were members of the manor court to compensation; but the right of subtenants, cottagers and squatters without manorial rights to retain access to common land and fen by established local custom was contentious. If anything, the government of Charles I was marginally more tender of the rights of this last group than was the Rump or the Protector. Where the poor took the law into their own hands to protest against drainage operations, for example, a detachment of the New Model Army was likely to be sent down and quartered in the area until the work of the contractors was completed. When even this failed, as at Swaffham Bulbeck in Cambridgeshire in 1653, the local military commander tried to press for the Navy 100 of those he suspected of vandalizing the drains and dykes.

The second prong of the reformers' pleas for land reform was for an end to inheritance by primogeniture. Nothing made English society so fluid and open as the way in which the bulk of the resources throughout the upper and middling ranks was handed on through the eldest son, creating massive downward social mobility in every generation, as those born into one social group were forced to adapt to the life-style of a lower social group. The younger sons of gentlemen and yeomen became tenant farmers, attorneys, merchants or craftsmen who tried to claw their way back to the status of their birth; the younger sons of husbandmen became labourers (and would try usually in vain to claw their way back). Not surprisingly, there was a campaign waged principally by younger sons (including most of the Leveller leaders) against 'the most unreasonable descent of inheritance to the eldest son only'. Parliaments dominated by the beneficiaries of the existing system listened and did nothing.

But in a third area, the situation of a particular group of farmers seems to have changed dramatically over this period. Between 1600 and 1700 a majority of all farms ceased to be held by copyhold and were changed into leasehold. Although much more detailed work needs to be done on this question, it seems likely that much of this change took place in the mid-seventeenth century. It was in the self-interest of most copyholders to convert their holdings into freehold. This would not only confirm and strengthen their own and their descendants' interest in the land; it would remove the hazards of periodic entry fines and other incidental charges. The landlord, on the other hand, was likely to wish to change copyholds into leases which gave him a certain and predictable rent rather than a low annual rent and unpredictable 'fines'. It seems that the landlords won.

Forms of tenure

In seventeenth-century England, there were a bewildering variety of ways in which landlords could rent out their lands to working farmers. The basic distinction was between *customary tenures* (often known as *copyholds*) and fixed-term tenancies (*leaseholds*). Copyholders were those who were tenants by virtue of the copy they possessed of an entry on the manorial roll, a copy which laid down the terms and conditions of the tenancy. Most such tenancies date back to the fifteenth century, and since the rents were fixed and immutable, tenants appeared to benefit in an age of inflation such as the century and more before the Interregnum. But the landlord had the right to collect a fee (known as an *entry fine*) every time the tenancy changed hands. In some areas the fine itself was fixed by custom, in others by the manor court, and in many more by the lord. Before 1640 the courts were able and willing to restrain greedy landlords who were unreasonable in levying fines. The campaign on behalf of copyholders in the 1640s was a campaign to abolish or commute entry fines, so that tenants simply paid the small annual rents and otherwise were free from charges and free to bequeath and sell their tenancies. Such a system left landlords unable to rationalize their estates and with very uncertain returns from any investment they might make, and they therefore preferred leaseholds, contracts for stated periods at fixed rents. Landlords could make contracts for one year at a time (*rackrenting*) but this created instability and was not worth the effort. Paradoxically, secure leases benefited both lords and tenants, since the lord had an incentive to invest in improvement, taking part of the much increased profit from the land in increased rents.

Several factors worked against the peasant farmer in the revolutionary decades. Tenants of Royalist landowners found themselves subject to local committees that confiscated manorial rolls and sought to maximize revenues by failing to renew old agreements and instead letting the land on an annual basis (or 'rackrent'). Landlords, on regaining their estates, claimed (on occasion no doubt genuinely) that their manorial records had not been recovered and that they had to make new agreements on a new basis. Tenants had hitherto been able to call on the protection of the equity courts (especially Chancery and Requests) to safeguard their interests. But in 1641 the Court of Requests was abolished, and in the early years of the Interregnum Chancery was barely functioning (the Nominated Assembly in 1653 briefly abolished it altogether). Tenants therefore had no easy way of withstanding landlord pressure. Equally importantly, the pressure to hold out against change was significantly reduced. There was an unprecedented mobility of farmers in the wake of the war. Many smallholders were away fighting and others seized the opportunity to take up vacant farms where they had fought rather than return home (as a detailed study of the many men from the Welsh borders settling in Dorset has shown). On the Verney estates in Buckinghamshire, the turnover of tenants was four times higher than in the decades before the Civil War. Tenants under landlord pressure shopped around looking for better deals elsewhere. The new taxation also weakened the benefits of copyhold over leasehold. Copyhold tenants had to bear the full weight of the assessment (property tax) on their holdings; while leaseholders shared the expense with their landlords.

If there was a major transition at this time, it would help to explain the chorus of demands in pamphlets and petitions for Parliament to secure the interests of copyholders, normally by allowing the tenancies to be converted to freehold by the payment of a lump sum in composition. The Levellers were in the forefront of this campaign to have copyhold 'the ancient and almost antiquated badge of slavery . . . (being the Conqueror's marks on the people) taken away'. The plea fell on deaf ears. Until a lot more detailed work has been completed, it is difficult to be sure, but it seems likely that between 1640 and 1660 copyholds were being converted to leasehold at an unprecedented rate. The English Revolution, by contrast with the French Revolution, liberated the greater landowners and made possible the great leap forward in agriculture over the next 200 years.

VIII

Most of the new farming technologies, new crops and new rotations were imported into England from the Netherlands. The experience of Royalist exiles in the 1650s in learning about these developments and pioneering them upon their return is a very obvious, if very oblique, consequence of the Revolution. A series of developments made it much more worth while for landlords to invest in the improvement of their estates. The first was the creation in the 1650s of new and even more rigid arrangements (known as 'strict settlements') for the inheritance of land. This made landowners more like trustees of family property which they could not sell without a private Act of Parliament, but which they were bound to hand on intact to their own eldest sons. The second was the development of a more sophisticated and secure mortgage market. The third was the consolidation of leasehold at the expense of copyhold. Under the latter, with low rents and uncertain entry fines (and other incidental payments) it was difficult to determine what return would be available on any investment. Landowners and leaseholders, on the other hand, could enter into formal arrangements by which each party knew what the other had to invest and what each stood to gain by increased yields and increased rents. Finally, the abolition of feudal dues meant that landowners no longer needed to fear that the Crown would asset-strip an estate in the event of it passing from father to son before the son came of age.

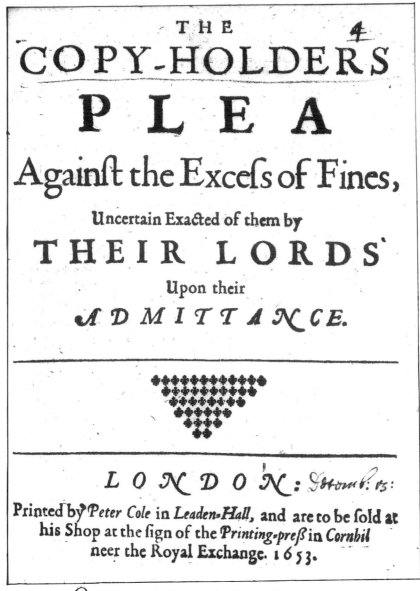

THE
COPY-HOLDERS
PLEA

Againſt the Exceſs of Fines,

Uncertain Exacted of them by

THEIR LORDS

Upon their

ADMITTANCE.

LONDON: Octomb: 15:

Printed by *Peter Cole* in *Leaden-Hall*, and are to be ſold at his Shop at the ſign of the *Printing-preſs* in *Cornhil* neer the Royal Exchange. 1653.

One of the tracts pleading for the small copyhold farmers who were under renewed pressure as landlords sought to make good their losses in the wars.

All these changes were directly or indirectly related to the political crisis of the 1640s and 1650s. What made them critically important was that the new opportunities coincided with a pause in the long-term upward cycle of population. Between 1640 and 1740 the population of England ceased to grow. The civil wars themselves may have contributed to this through the high death rate in battle and more especially in diseases borne by marching armies; through a birth rate lowered by the long absences of significant numbers of young soldiers on campaign; and in the 1650s through the highest emigration rate before the nineteenth century (no doubt encouraged by the war-related economic crises of the later 1640s). Well over 10,000 younger people were voluntarily migrating each year to the West Indies and the American mainland, and the State was transporting others as a penalty for sedition or for being among the able-bodied poor. But other factors – including a later age of marriage and a consequent lower fertility rate for women – were at work, keeping population levels stable until they began to climb again in the second quarter of the eighteenth century. This affected the pattern of agricultural investment. In the early seventeenth century that investment had taken the form of exploiting cheap labour costs by extending the amount of land under the plough and by the introduction of new labour-intensive crops such as dye-crops and mulberry trees (for the worms that would allow for the development of a native silk industry). In contrast, the period after 1660 saw a concentration on new technology and new rotations which increased yields. These were capital-intensive rather than labour-intensive developments.

IX

The impact of the Revolution on the land was therefore to help the large landowner in reorganizing his vast estates into family-sized farms which were leased out and efficiently modernized. The impact on urban society is more difficult to assess. The Civil War certainly freed some parts of the urban economy. The urgent need for mass production of certain goods during the war years – shoes for the soldiers is an obvious example – helped to bring about the collapse of guild regulation in many towns; as did the demobilization of many soldiers who were granted parliamentary exemption from serving full apprenticeships before setting up small shops and workshops. The mass market provided by armies may also have accelerated the process of regional specialization – such as the Northampton shoe industry. Once again, as in their defence of the small peasant producer in the countryside, the attempt of the Levellers to protect the interests of the small producer in the towns (above all their hostility to entrepreneurs and to a separation of producer from the market) shows them to have been economically regressive.

The Navigation Acts of 1651 (and the 1660s) which gave a monopoly to English merchants in importing and re-exporting colonial goods as well as supplying various important markets may have created a protective umbrella which allowed greater competition among English merchants at the same time as it excluded foreign rivals. But in terms of urban society it is more difficult to see any major shift as a result of the Interregnum. Religious toleration probably led to separatist activity sinking deeper roots in towns

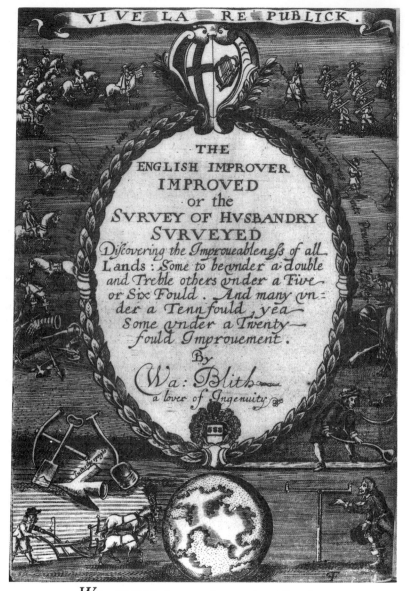

Walter Blith's The Improver Improved *went through many editions in the 1650s and incorporated all the best Dutch schemes for land improvement.*

than in the countryside, roots which could not be grubbed up by the stuttering persecution of Restoration regimes. It certainly led to the development of a high proportion of the economically dominant families in many towns developing a commitment to religious forms incompatible with Anglican practice, so that the attempts to remove Nonconformists in the early 1660s were but briefly effective. But the other developments in seventeenth-century urban history (the decline of the smaller boroughs and the consolidation of the regional capitals as centres of marketing, services and entertainment) were all well established as trends before 1640.

X

After the violence and strife of the 1640s, the Interregnum was a surprisingly quiet time. Despite the war of words over social injustice (and many other forms of injustice), levels of public violence were probably lower in the 1650s than in any earlier decade. Traditional forms of protest (enclosure riot, grain riot) ebbed away, and the characteristic forms of civilian protest of the 1640s (confrontations with soldiers, iconoclasm, defence of the local community against outsiders) vanished. While some radical religious groups – notably the Quakers – engaged in campaigns of civil disobedience (organizing tithe strikes, disrupting religious services conducted by their public enemies), even they sought only to prick the soft underbelly of Cromwell's religious liberalism rather than indulge in violent confrontation. Even the collection of the new and onerous forms of taxation – above all excise – failed to provoke major outbursts of public violence once the State realized the need to avoid the flashpoint of levying it at the point of sale.

There was then an almost complete absence of widespread enclosure riots, grain riots, tithe riots or tax riots throughout the 1650s. 'Moral force' religious movements which eschewed violence found that they had to endure it. 'Moral force' movements could create moral panics, as the great Quaker Fear of 1659 – which was the mirror image of the great Catholic panic of 1641 – demonstrates. But in terms of men and women killed, heads broken, property looted and destroyed, the 1650s was one of the least disordered decades in English history.

Interregnum social history is a whirligig of ideas; but it was a time of considerable peace for those who feared the collapse of order. One can count in dozens the numbers of Diggers who sought to reclaim the common land for the common people; or the number of those called Ranters who sought publicly to flout Christian morality as it had been taught by and enjoined by the orthodox preachers. Ann Hughes and Patricia Crawford both have important things to say about this in their essays in this volume.

The Interregnum was a period in which more people joined in debates about government. The franchise reforms of the Instrument of Government probably reduced by one-third those entitled to vote in parliamentary elections (once again the call of the Levellers for a massive extension of the franchise, perhaps so as to include all adult males went unheeded and, after 1649, largely unremembered). But there was certainly more opportunity for the unenfranchised to find out about politics, to debate religious ideas, to take part in petitioning movements and mass demonstrations (at least in the towns). The dissemination of news and of thousands of inexpensive pamphlets must have had an effect on that generation; the opportunity to listen to itin-erant preachers, the encouragement to read the scriptures and to form one's own conclusions, are an important part of the experience of this period. It seems likely that the bureaucracy of local government – the hordes of assessors, collectors, commissioners over and above the traditional officers of the civil parish (the constables, overseers and churchwardens) – spread responsibility more widely than ever before, especially among those groups on the margins of literacy. For the middling sort, the role of the grand jury at quarter sessions and assizes, assisting the justices and judges in the work of county government, may have been enhanced. In Cheshire, for example, we find grand juries made up of substantial farmers and men in the grey area separating the gentry and the yeomanry criticizing the JPs as a whole for their failure to carry out their duties properly and even telling the assize judges who ought to be added to the commission of the peace.

In the long run, this ferment may have mattered little. The Restoration was a restoration of gentry power even more than it was a restoration of king and bishop. Censorship was back and it was a generation before information was again as freely disseminated as it had been in the 1650s. Mass petitioning – except firmly under gentry supervision – was prohibited. Although tens of thousands avoided their parish church and quietly worshipped in a conventicle, the fervour and ferment of the 1650s was largely spent. Enthusiasm was a dirty word in Restoration England.

XI

It was the nobility and greater gentry who were to emerge with the ability to develop more flexible ways of gaining wealth and power. In a way, the tremendous scare they had had bound them more tightly together. Thomas Hobbes and the Earl of Clarendon had little in common intellectually; but both argued that one cause of the Civil War had been an over-educated populace. The Restoration was to see a de-emphasis on the merits of teaching all and sundry which was to last for a century. The franchise was gradually to decline from the figure of one in three males which it had been shown had the right to vote in the decades before 1649; this proportion was not regained until 1885. Fear of revolution from below constrained those engaged in the power struggle of 1678–81 and helped the centre to hold in 1688–9 so that the militants spoiling for a fight were thwarted. The fudge represented by the Bill of Rights was an important ingredient in persuading the élite to compromise.

The English Revolution of 1649 was not a social revolution in the sense that it did not change the social system or the social distribution of wealth and power. It affected society *negatively* more obviously than it affected society *positively*. It probably deepened gentry neu-rosis about 'the many-headed monster'. As they struggled to make good their losses, it almost certainly reduced gentry paternalism and altruism. It is from the Restoration that game parks, gamekeepers and game laws proliferate. It is from the late seventeenth century that the wealthy start moving their houses away from a dominating proximity to the village communities or even (as at Houghton or Wimpole) pulled down and moved the village. Between 1450 and 1650 the proportion of land held in estates of more than 10,000 acres (4,000 hectares) had remained at between 10 and 15 per cent; by 1750 it had risen to about 25 per cent. Estates of less than 300 acres had slumped from 35 to 20 per cent. Yet while this was happening, tens of thousands – and perhaps hundreds of thousands – of men and women opted out of their parish churches. Since the gentry were never able to compel them back into it, a new freedom of choice opened up for anyone stifled by the squire-and-parson alliance.

The English Revolution consolidated the élite when it might have destroyed it; consolidated order by giving everyone a taste of, and distaste for, disorder; prepared the way for the collapse of the confessional State while discrediting the Puritan dream of the godly commonwealth; and created, by the law of unintended consequences, new opportunities for wealth and investment. In changing attitudes rather than structures, creating its own myths which those who lived through it taught their children and their children's children, the Revolution of 1649 lived on.

CHAPTER VI

The Challenges to Patriarchalism: How did the Revolution affect Women?

PATRICIA CRAWFORD

I Introduction and historiography

Every society takes account of difference of sex, in that gender order of one kind or another exists in every society. Western Europe societies in the early modern period can be described as patriarchal, in the sense that fathers or men generally had social advantages. The belief that God had ordained this rule of male over female was fundamental to social organization. The female sex was assumed to be inferior, and therefore to be subordinate.

Historians have only recently become interested in analysing the effects of difference of sex on social organization and experience. Previously, they accepted the nineteenth-century distinction between the public and the private spheres. Historians wrote as though they believed that women, belonging as they did to the household, had lived through history in some kind of timeless present, eternally bearing and rearing children and running households. Women had no history. Politics, on the other hand, was in the public sphere. Politics was men's business, and the proper stuff of historical analysis. Since the majority of historians were (and are) male, such views were not widely disputed. Consequently, despite enormous interest in the English civil wars and Interregnum, questions about their significance for women have not often been raised or discussed. There is not a large historiography on the effects of the revolutionary decades upon women, although such pioneering work as there is can be found listed in the notes for further reading (see pages 152–3).

In an article about the effect of the civil wars on women, Keith Thomas examined the effects of their participation in the radical religious sects of those years. Although contemporaries were deeply disturbed by women's radical religious activity, Thomas concluded that in the long run it had little influence on the position of women in English society:

> Nor does the sectarian insistence upon women's spiritual equality seem to have been of very great importance in the later history of female emancipation in general . . . [F]or the most part, future feminist movements were to base their arguments less upon any renewed assertion of women's spiritual equality than upon natural right and the denial of any intellectual differences between the sexes.

Thomas's conclusion has been broadly repeated subsequently by other historians, whose interests, admittedly, were more in the family than in women. For example, Ralph Houlbrooke, writing of the effects of the revolutionary period upon the family, concluded that 'even among the minority which experienced female religious radicalism it did not bring about a major redistribution of power within the family.' Christopher Durston agreed that while the absolute authority of husbands and fathers was questioned during the years 1640–60,

> these years saw only the tentative opening rounds of a long contest to establish greater rights and freedoms for wives and children. In addition, any discrediting of patriarchy which did occur during these years probably owed as much to the assumption by wives of greater duties and responsibilities, and to the mutual support that many spouses brought to each other in the face of external danger, as it did to conflict and ideological discord.

In this chapter, I wish to discuss the impact of the English revolution on women. Did women really assume 'greater duties and responsibilities' during the Revolution, and did this discredit patriarchy, as Durston suggests? How did women's participation in the radical religious sects affect their social situations? To what extent was patriarchy questioned during the Revolution? Politically, Charles was executed as an errant King. At his trial, the right of fathers to rule was never questioned. Few people accepted that the rule of the father was over. Certainly no man thought that the rule of men over women and families was abrogated. Even the radical Gerrard Winstanley, when he reviewed more sensible ways of performing household tasks in his ideal society, thought that the housework of a hundred women could be done by twenty-five. It is important to note that housework was still women's work. To question the gender division of labour would really have turned the world upside down.

II Continuities

1 Sexuality

The first point to stress is that the Revolution did not alter any of the fundamental constraints on women's lives. If a woman engaged in sexual activity, she risked pregnancy. No reliable contraceptives were known and, while there has been much talk of 'folk remedies', none was so widely known or effective as to prevent unmarried women from facing severe penalties for bastard-bearing. Married women continued to bear children about every two years, hence, for much of their lives after their mid-twenties, they were likely to be either pregnant or lactating. Childbearing and rearing remained central to women's lives during the Revolution.

Contemporaries believed that religious radicalism in the 1640s and 1650s was a cover for sexual disorder. Heresiographers said that women joined sects for the sake of sexual liberty. The hysterical writings of Thomas Edwards and others made all the sectaries appear

Child-bearing and child-rearing remained central to women's lives.

to be engaged in undercover sexual promiscuity. Contemporaries were convinced that the Revolution led to sexual licence and several historians, including Christopher Hill, have to a degree agreed. But while contemporaries grew frenzied at the thought of 'Base impudent kisses' in the sects, what is known about the conduct of separatist congregations shows that the social discipline there was stricter than anywhere else.

From The Rangers Ranting *(1650), one of many tracts which alleged that the sects were a cover for sexual promiscuity.*

When we consider the question of female sexuality during the English Revolution, it is important to remember that, for women, sex always had the possibility of reproduction. They believed that any sexual encounter, at any stage of their menstrual cycle, could lead to pregnancy. Consequently, women's attitudes to sex were affected by the possibility of pregnancy. Nothing changed about this during the Revolution. Gerrard Winstanley was one of the few radicals who recognized that sexual freedom was only a possibility for men; women were still left with the babies.

Furthermore, far from an increase in extra-marital or illicit sexuality during the Revolution, the evidence suggests that the reverse was the case. Certainly there was less tolerance of illicit sexual activity. Parliament passed a Draconian act in 1650 against sexual activity outside marriage. Nevertheless, despite some limited attempts by Puritan magistrates and radicals to review the double standard of sexual morality, the penalties for men and women differed. Any

115

married woman who had sexual relations with any man other than her husband was to be put to death for adultery. Married men who had sex outside marriage were guilty only of fornication, which carried a lesser penalty.

The 1650s were not a decade of sexual liberty for women. At a time when magistrates were endeavouring to enforce a strict code of morality, the ratio of illegitimate births to legitimate ones was at its lowest level for the whole of the seventeenth century. Women were still punished for what the law called bastard-bearing. Since they had fewer financial resources than men, and since many were servants who were seduced in the households of their masters and then dismissed on becoming pregnant, they were more likely to suffer the physical punishments of a whipping and confinement to the house of correction than their male partner. Men were more likely to be discharged with a fine and the maintenance of the child, if it lived. Furthermore, while it is not surprising that the testimonies of unmarried women to the magistrates do not celebrate sexual pleasure, the evidence in many cases tells of women's fear, and of men's force which frequently amounted to rape.

There was an observed change in the sexual mores of the court after the Restoration, when Charles II and his prominent courtiers publicly flaunted their sexual exploits. Female courtiers, after over a century of security from the sexual advances of the reigning monarch, found themselves vulnerable. Many historians have seen the King's promiscuity as part of the 'merry monarch' image but, from the women's point of view, it may have been sexual harassment. The gentlewomen who worked at the court for the usual rewards of place and patronage for themselves and their families found that compliance with male sexual demands outside marriage was part of the public face of court culture.

How the sexual mores of the Restoration court relate to the revolutionary decades is a difficult and intriguing problem. The question has been little discussed by historians, although literary critics and cultural historians have been more interested. The obvious point would be to argue that the aristocratic men and women were reacting to the repression of the 1640s and 1650s, but this seems too simple. Charles II may have been reacting to his father's austere morality and authority rather than to any public events in England. Furthermore, post-Restoration sexual licentiousness had a class dimension. Its public enjoyment was limited to those men who could afford to maintain a mistress and their illegitimate children. At a lower social level, the Quarter Sessions were still summoning men who fathered illegitimate children and requiring them to pay for maintenance, and punishing women who bore bastards. Finally, sexual licentiousness may have been more pleasurable for men than for women. The post-Restoration discovery of the sperm under the microscope altered medical theories about the process of conception. Whereas earlier medical theorists had popularized the notion that female sexual pleasure was necessary for the conception of a child, the theory that the child was preformed in the sperm or the ovum seemed to make female orgasms irrelevant to reproductive purposes.

2 Work

Most women's lives continued to be affected by their need to get a livelihood during the revolutionary decades and afterwards. While the husbands of married women were expected to contribute the bulk of cash to a household, wives were expected to run the household and to supply many of its needs by their labour. There were regional variations in women's work and some differences between town and country. But in all places there was a sexual division of labour. In addition to responsibility for children and the household, women spun wool and made clothing; they managed dairies and produced butter and cheese which they sold at market; they provided the labour force needed at harvest time. In cities, much

---

Quaker women against tithes, 1659

It may seem strange to some that women should appear in so publick a manner, in a matter of so great concernment as this of Tithes, and wee also should bring in our testimony even as our brethren against that Anti–Christian law and oppression of tithes, by which many of the servants of the Lord have suffered in filthy holes and dungeons until death; But let such know, that this is the work of the Lord at this day, even by weak means to bring to pass his mighty work in the earth, that all flesh may be silent, and the Lord alone may be exalted in them who can truly say, Now I live, yet not I, but Christ liveth in me . . . ; Behold our God is appearing for us, and they that be in the light may see him, choosing the foolish things of the World to confound the wise, weak things to confound the Mighty, vile things, and things that are despised hath God chosen, ye and things which are not, to bring to nought things which are; . . .

And Christ did provide another maintenance for his Ministers and Disciples then Tithes . . . The true Church is coming out of the Wilderness again, and the Beast as the false prophet cast alive into the lake of fire, and the Judgment of the great Whore is come, the false church; The Lamb, the Saints shall have the victory, the Lamb, the Bride is known again, preparing for her husbands coming out of the Wilderness, and the daughters of Abraham are meeting of her, who gives in their Testimony against this oppressive Church, Ministry and maintenance . . .

These several papers was sent to the Parliament . . . Being above seven thousand of the names of the Hand-Maids and Daughters of the Lord.
Printed for Mary Westwood, 1659, pp. 1, 38–9.

of the sale of perishable foodstuffs was in female hands. None of this changed during the Revolution, although getting a livelihood may have been more difficult because of the disruption of the wars.

The rise of the professions continued to restrict women's opportunities to engage in more lucrative work. Despite movements during the revolutionary period for knowledge to be freely available to all, the consolidation of male professional groups disadvantaged women, especially in medicine and health care. Physicians ridiculed women's knowledge, dismissing it as harmful to patients. In the area of midwifery, women's attempts to secure better training were frustrated, and the clerical licensing authorities continued to prefer a good character and Anglican conformity to anatomical knowledge. While many women midwives continued to enjoy a successful practice based on their experience and skill, the rise of the man-midwife was obvious by the end of the seventeenth century. Upper-class women were the first to choose to employ men for this function.

III Changes

1 *Intensification of existing roles*

Some women's roles did not change during the civil wars and Interregnum, although changes could best be described as the intensification of existing roles. During this period, many husbands were away fighting and wives perforce became heads of households. Gentlewomen and ladies had always been required to manage estates in the absence of husbands, discussing leases and farming with stewards and bailiffs. The wars placed further demands, as many men were away in Parliament, with armies, or in exile. During the 1640s some women defended their houses against enemy forces.

During the 1650s, many Royalist gentlewomen were forced to appear before committees to plead for estates and to negotiate composition fines. Some, like Margaret Cavendish, Countess of Newcastle, may have found this distasteful, but she pleaded her case successfully. Nor was the example of Royalist women lost upon their female contemporaries. As Bathsua Makin observed in 1673,

> in these late Times there are several instances of Women, when their Husbands were serving their King and Countrey, defended their Houses, and did all things, as Souldiers, with Prudence and Valour, like Men. They appeared before Committees, and pleaded their own Causes with good success.

Furthermore, as executors of husbands' wills, widows were required to account for large sums of money collected for the public coffers. For example, one female executrix, Elizabeth Herring, joined with Richard Waring in swearing to the accounts in 1660 for delinquents' and recusants' lands worth over £1.6 million.

Middling women were involved in the defence of cities and towns. Some acted as spies, messengers and go-betweens. They were ideally suited to such work because they attracted less suspicion than men as they moved around. Women were also required to nurse wounded soldiers. Among the women of middling status, some worked as contractors for Army supplies. Some women in the country endeavoured to support one side or the other, while others struggled to survive against marauders and to feed their families.

The numbers of women in poverty probably increased during the wars. Since it was assumed that men's wages were necessary for a household, and women's work was always paid less than men's, the deaths and injuries of husbands and fathers forced women to look after their families with inadequate resources. In many areas the collection of poor rates was disrupted. At all social levels, women petitioned whenever they could for help, some for their husbands' arrears of pay or for pensions. There was an increase in social distress during the 1650s. Because of the disorder of the wars, magistrates were more concerned about women outside patriarchal authority. During the 1650s they tried to enforce earlier legislation, ordering women as well as men to go into service where they would be under the authority of a master. There was nothing especially new about any of this. Increased poverty and government alarm were the normal effects of a crisis such as war, harvest failure or plague. Any economic crisis could force women into a variety of expedients for their own survival and that of their children. Women's work patterns did not alter during or after the revolutionary period. They were still limited in access to employment, and were still paid lower wages.

2 Religion and radicalism

The main effect of the English Revolution on women was in providing greater opportunities for them to express their ideas individually and collectively. Their public statements of their views enhanced female self-confidence; women were more prepared to publish challenges to patriarchal power at the end of the seventeenth century than they were a century earlier. It could also be argued that, in response to women's increasing assertiveness, men sought to restrict female independence and female access to a public voice.

The greatest single force influencing women's social situation in the revolutionary decades was their religious beliefs. During the 1640s and 1650s ideas changed rapidly, especially ideas about authority and religious belief. Publications from the press increased dramatically and, although fewer women than men were literate, they were part of the wider audience who read or heard new ideas. Public debate intensified, but although MPs were alarmed at the spread of discussion of political issues outside the House, they could do little to confine it. They were especially disturbed at stories of women preaching, teaching and prophesying.

Religious belief was the key to much of women's radical activity during the 1640s and 1650s. From at least the time of the Protestant

Reformation in England, women had been authorized to disobey an unbelieving husband for the sake of the true faith. While it was largely the Protestant wives of Catholic husbands whom the Reformers were supporting, the principle of resistance was nevertheless established. For the sake of her faith, a woman should defy all earthly authority.

Many women were critical of the established Anglican Church and after 1640 took seriously Parliament's promises of a reformation of religion. Some, dissatisfied with existing churches, formed small groups, searching together for salvation. Separatist churches often developed out of such groups, in which women usually outnumbered men. Religious sects multiplied and, from the beginning, women were prominent in witnessing, even in teaching and preaching. Sectarian women were only a minority in London and a few other cities, but they shocked and horrified ministers and other men in authority out of all proportion to their numbers. Women as well as men helped to create an environment in which radicalism flourished.

Women preachers were not unknown before 1640, but they had been punished and were few in number. During the 1640s and 1650s, women were in less danger for their words because the ecclesiastical courts were abolished and, by the time the Presbyterian Church was substituted for the Anglican, the reality of religious pluralism and separatism made control impossible. Apart from the more sustained preaching by Quaker women, much of the women's speech about religion was in the form of interruptions in churches, or messages to magistrates, or participation in smaller religious groups in private houses.

Prophecy was another form of public female speech on important public issues. Denied access to the more conventional opportunities open to men for making their views known, such as Parliament or the pulpit, women turned to prophecy. This was a form of speech which seemed particularly suited to women, since it involved the abnegation of self to become a vessel of the Lord. Female prophets argued that they were merely instruments of the Lord, but their conservative rhetoric disguised their radical actions. Women prophets included the Fifth Monarchists Mary Cary, who wrote of an ideal society, the new Jerusalem, and Anna Trapnel, whose prophecies criticized the rule of the rich, including that of Oliver Cromwell, and urged the claims of the poor. Phyllis Mack has identified over 300 women prophets in the two decades of the Revolution. The prophecies of some of these women – such as Cary, Trapnel, Elizabeth Poole, Sara Wight and others – were published, and thus the female voice reached a wider audience.

Women's participation in the Quaker movement in the 1650s shows how female radicalism was linked with religious beliefs. Quakerism developed from small groups of women and men around England and Wales. The preaching of George Fox and others joined the groups into a powerful movement. Some women, such as

*W*omen *were allowed some freedom to preach among the Quakers*
but not at all amongst other sects, and even among the Quakers were
treated with doubt and suspicion.

Elizabeth Hooton, were also preachers. Others undertook missionary
journeys to the cities and towns of England and even abroad. In the
service of the truth, Quaker women denounced ministers in what the
Quakers contemptuously called 'steeple houses' in time of worship.
Many Quaker women were set upon by angry crowds.

In preaching the message, Quaker women showed initiative,
imagination and courage. A few chose to enact public dramas
to draw attention to their message. Thus, like some Quaker men,
they went 'naked for a sign' and tried to show by their rejection of

outward covering that all people were basically sinful. One woman from Kent brought a large earthenware tub which she set outside the Parliament house, standing upon it to address the passers-by, and turning it around with various pertinent observations, such as that the world was now a-turning.

Most significantly of all, some women challenged the Quaker male leadership. In 1656 Martha Simmonds tried to preach the message she had received from the Lord in Quaker meetings in London. Angrily, the male London leaders told her to be quiet, because her message was not the Lord's message. But Simmonds was not persuaded and turned to one of the leaders, James Nayler, to support her. Initially Nayler was unsympathetic, telling her to go home and 'meddle with your housewifery'. Simmonds went home, but felt the power of the Lord rise in her. After three days, Nayler was convinced: Simmonds's power was from God. Subsequently Nayler took part in a major drama in Bristol, when he participated in a re-enactment of Christ's entry into Jerusalem which was designed to warn the citizens of their sinfulness. For his part in this, Nayler was savagely punished. The women who were involved were initially questioned for being witches or whores but, in the end, escaped punishment, no doubt because the authorities believed that women were accessories to crimes, not initiators. Simmonds continued to try to lead in Quaker worship. She read prophecies and went so far as to offer bread and drink to a Quaker meeting at the Bull and Mouth Tavern. Since Quakers did not believe in the formal administration of the sacraments, her action was unwelcome. To other Christians at that date, the idea that a woman could exercise the sacred function of offering the bread and wine was horrifying.

Memories of female disorder were among the most troubling legacies of the revolutionary decades. In 1659 the Duke of Newcastle was convinced of the need for social control. He explained to Charles II that the education of lower-class women, as well of lower-class men, was a mistake: 'the Bible in English under every weaver's and chambermaid's arms hath done us much hurt.' Records from the 1650s confirm his fears about the dangers of reading. For example, in 1650 Elizabeth Townshend, a member of an Independent church, failed to attend public worship on the Lord's day, and spent her time instead with young men and women in 'foolish discourse'. One man read out of a book 'called the flying rowle', which was presumably Abeizer Coppe's radical pamphlet, *A Fiery Flying Roll*, published a few months earlier. This book, 'full of cursed swearing and horrid blasphemies', led to 'much foolish laughter among them', but Elizabeth carried the book away with her. She was unabashed when her church threatened to cast her out, arguing 'That the Church was no Church for God's love was alike to all'. Like other religious radicals, she rejected the notion of the Church as a formal body with a fixed membership. The opportunity to read about different ideas and to discuss alternatives had led her to defy the norms of submissive female behaviour and of religious conformity.

Women were a significant presence in all the separatist churches, frequently outnumbering men by as many as two to one. The male leaders were always troubled at signs of female independence. Sexual politics existed in the separatist churches as ministers and elders attempted to control women's participation. The ministers found themselves caught between the critics of the sects, who feared female disorder, and the women in their congregations who challenged their rule. The independence which took women into separatist congregations was unwelcome once the women were accepted as members. Good women in a separatist church were expected to be subordinate and obedient.

The religious radicals were, however, a minority, and the majority of women were probably pleased when the King returned in 1660. The Restoration seemed to signal a return to order and known ways. However, for many religious groups, the Restoration brought about an unhappy change. The Presbyterians and Independents found themselves numbered among the sectaries and persecuted for their beliefs.

Women were essential to Nonconformity. Indeed, without their support it is hard to see how it could have survived at all, since the women numbered at last half the congregations. After 1660 the Dissenters endured persecution and, after toleration at the end of the century, they made few converts. The congregations depended upon the children of believers to continue the faith. Here the role of household religion and female piety was vital. Mothers who taught their children on a daily basis about the importance of their faith ensured the perpetuation of Nonconformity. Although much attention has been focused on the ministers and their heroic endurance of imprisonment after 1660, the long-term significance of female commitment was far greater. The endurance of the minister himself frequently depended upon the moral support of his wife.

The Quakers were less affected by the Restoration than other Dissenters. They had been persecuted before, so the experience of suffering was not new. Yet, in the end, they were forced as a movement to respond and to organize to protect themselves against fines, distraint of goods and the consequences of their refusal to observe certain conventions such as the swearing of oaths in court. Some Quaker organization affected the roles of women. Female preaching was questioned and there was a major split in the movement in the 1670s over the role of women's separate meetings. All writings for publications were considered by a committee of men and increasingly, as the Quakers sought to antagonize other people less, so the prophetic and wilder writings – where women had been prominent – were censored.

After 1660, a process known as denominationalization was at work and women's conduct in the Nonconformist churches was more restricted. The sects became more organized, in response to the demands of the world. They insisted on greater moral purity and piety to set themselves apart from the world. In general, religious enthusiasm was feared, satirized and repressed. Male leaders of Nonconformist churches could not be insensitive to this. In the quest for some degree of respectability, they endeavoured to suppress what they saw as the 'wilder' manifestations of female spirituality.

Yet, for all this, the existence of Nonconformity after 1660 allowed women greater religious choice. There were religious alternatives, and the numbers of women in the separatist congregations showed that these alternatives were proportionately more attractive to them than to men. For all the limitations which the male leaders attempted to impose upon female participation, Dissenting congregations offered women a great opportunity to engage in Church business. Women participated in choosing ministers and in the decisions to admit members. Women continued to express their views by speaking, writing and even voting. No such opportunities were afforded by the Anglican Church so, in this respect, women had gained by the experiences of the revolutionary decades.

Thus a Dissenting or Nonconformist tradition was established in England which continues to the present day. The presence of this critical tradition, which women played a vital role in sustaining, was fundamental to the development of religious toleration and parliamentary democracy.

3 Enhanced female self-confidence: individual and collective voices of women

During the 1640s and 1650s, a few women seized the greater opportunities to speak out in public. They preached, prophesied and published. They took advantage of conditions of greater freedom to express their views both as individuals and collectively. Furthermore, nearly all the women who published their writings as individuals were conscious of themselves as women, as were those who acted collectively in petitioning Parliament. Female self-confidence was enhanced. By their participation in religious radicalism and public debate women helped to make the Revolution.

The 1640s and 1650s saw an enormous increase in the number of publications by women. This expansion was not just part of the general increase in publication after the collapse of the censorship through Star Chamber. Women's publications increased as a proportion of total publications in the 1640s and 1650s, constituting about 1.2 per cent of total publications compared with 0.5 per cent before the wars. Furthermore, after 1640, women published in a wider range of genres than they had done earlier. Before 1640, women published religious works, plays, poems, literary pieces and maternal advice. After 1640 they published political treatises, almanacs, medical treatises and midwives' guides, prophecies and prose fictions. Especially significant was their intervention in political controversy for the first time. Although the five-year period of 1645 to 1649 remained the high

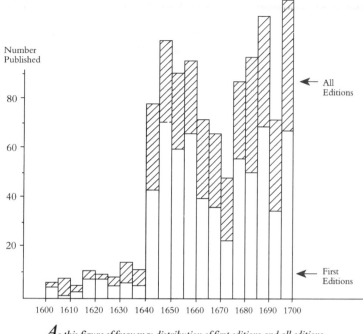

*As this figure of frequency distribution of first editions and all editions
of women's writings 1600-1700 illustrates, there was a decisive jump in
the 1640s and 1650s sustained down to the end of the century.*

point of their publishing activity during the seventeenth century, and
was not equalled in any other five-year period before 1700, the position of women as writers for the press was well established during the
second half of the century. Women had expanded the number of areas
in which their views were public and had increased in confidence as
writers. This evidence of increased participation in publication is one
of the strongest arguments for the long-term effects of the Revolution
on women. Writing brought women into a wider sphere of public
activity.

Immediately after the Restoration, total publications were fewer.
Women were publishing less, not only in numbers of books and
pamphlets, but proportionately less than men. However, it was
a temporary set-back. Women's writings never returned to the
pre-Civil War level of less than 0.5 per cent and, by the end
of the seventeenth century, women's publications were increasing
in number and range. A career as an author was a possibility, as
Aphra Behn's life demonstrated.

During the Revolution, women found a public collective voice. As
women, they organized public petitions. Initially, female petitioning
could be seen as an extension of the conventional rights of a subject
to petition Parliament. Parliament accepted women's petitions in the
early years when they supported the policies of the majority, but in
1649 women's petitions in support of the imprisoned Leveller leaders

Women's claim to political rights, May 1649

That since we are assured of our Creation in the image of God, and of an interest in Christ, equal unto men, as also of a proportionable share in the Freedoms of this Commonwealth, we cannot but wonder and grieve that we should appear so despicable in your eyes, as to be thought unworthy to Petition or represent our Grievances to this Honourable House. Have we not an equal interest with the men of this Nation in those liberties and securities contained in the Petition of Right and other good laws of the land? Are any of our lives, limbs, liberties, or goods to be taken from us more than from men, but by due process of law . . . ? And can you imagine us to be so sottish or stupid as not to perceive, or not to be sencible when dayly those strong defences of our peace and wellfare are broken down and trod underfoot by force and arbitrary power?

Would you have us kept at home in our houses, when men of such faithfulness and integrity as the four prisoners, our friends, are fetched out of their beds and forced from their houses by soldiers . . . ? . . . And are we Christians, and yet must we sit still and keep at home . . . and shall we shew no sence of their sufferings? . . . Let it be accounted folly, presumption, madness, or whatsoever in us, whilst we have life and breath, we will never leave them . . .

To the supreme authority [5 May 1649]

were unwelcome. Told to go home, the women returned a week later with a forcefully argued statement of their right as women to express their views in public. The women's petition of May 1649 marks a high point in women's claims to participate in politics. In 1653 Katherine Chidley petitioned Parliament on behalf of 6,000 women. Again, in 1659, the petition of Quaker women against tithes – 7,000 women, 'hand-maids of the Lord', it was claimed – represented a major feat of political organization. The hand-maids petitioned not just as Quakers but as women. The numbers involved were impressive and only some of the Leveller petitions may have attracted similar support.

IV Reflections on the effects of the Revolution

When men thought about the effects of the Revolution on women, the majority considered that female disorder was one of the worst features of the revolutionary period. Women had been uncontrolled. They had defied husbands and fathers for the sake of religious belief. They had disrupted worship in congregations. They had preached, they had published and they had prophesied. The Revolution may have made men more suspicious of women, more hostile to them.

But what did women think about the effects of the Revolution on them as a sex? Just as men thought about the effects of the Revolution on women, so too did women. This is not to argue that women's consciousness of themselves as a sex was a product of the Revolution. There is evidence from earlier periods that male misogyny had forced women to confront the 'problem' of their female identity. No woman could live her life indifferent to assumptions about the nature of the female sex. But during the Revolution the writing and public action by women contributed to the development of what might be called a feminist consciousness. At the end of the seventeenth century, Mary Astell had some sharp observations on the relative social positions of women and men:

> That the Custom of the World has put Women, generally speaking, into a State of Subjection, is not deny'd; but the Right can no more be prov'd from the Fact, than the Predominancy of Vice can justify it . . . Again, Men are possess'd of all Places of Power, Trust and Profit, they make Laws and exercise the Magistracy . . . [Women] think as humbly of themselves as their Masters can wish, with respect to the other Sex. . .
>
> If absolute authority be not necessary in a state, how comes it so in a family? Or, if in a family, why not in a state . . . Is it not then partial in men to the last degree to contend for and practise that arbitrary dominion in their families which they abhor and exclaim against in the state?

Rather less sophisticated but equally to the point was Hannah Wolley's observation in 1675 that men thought women designed for breeding and cleaning only: 'Vain man is apt to think we were merely intended for the Worlds propagation, and to keep its humane inhabitants sweet and clean.'

As we have seen, the Revolution intensified women's customary roles in a more public and visible way. Public action enhanced female self-confidence generally among middling- and upper-status women. Of course, women did not participate in the formal political arena. Although some had voted in parliamentary elections during the first half of the seventeenth century, there was no demand for any extension of the franchise to women, even though women were voting in some separatist churches. Nor were there any demands for increased female participation in local government. But, by taking common public action about some of the major issues of the day, some women had claimed the right to participate in politics, a claim of long-term significance.

In symbolic terms, the execution of the King, which could be described as the death of the patriarch, probably did not affect women's lives. The really radical political ideas expressed by women owe more to religious beliefs than to political theory about patriarchalism. The legacies of the Revolution for women were ideas and self-confidence. In the long run, women's interests depended on their own ideas and beliefs rather than those of men. Criticism of women's social situation over the centuries has come more from female consciousness in women's movements than from liberal rights' theorists. That is, the achievements of feminism to date have depended more on women's own ideas and activities than on the concessions men have made on the basis of liberal theory. Liberal theory, as feminist analysis and female experience have shown, offers only limited rights to women.

The effects of the radical experience, while it was confined to a minority of women, was enormously important to female consciousness. Religious radicalism provided women with a public opportunity to think, to argue and to act. There was, of course, a conservative backlash after the Restoration. By the end of the seventeenth century, new political theories had developed which disadvantaged women. Ideas about gender intersected with class structures and led to new rigidities and limitations on women chiefly in the middling and upper levels of society. Political thinkers who developed doctrines of rights chose to assume that these were inherent in male property owners. Men could be born with rights but could lose these because they undertook to serve others. Women who owned property were denied citizenship, and the fundamental problem posed by Mary Astell was never put on the agenda for debate, let alone resolved: 'If all Men are born free, how is it that all Women are born Slaves?' At the end of the century, women's voices were raised in protest: that a woman should obey every whim of her husband, said Mary Chudleigh, 'is a tyranny, I think, that extends further than the most absolute Monarchs in the World'. While such voices may have been few and men may have been deaf, the articulation of a feminist protest was important to women and the history of their struggle for social rights.

The conflicts of the years 1640–60 had allowed women to participate more in public affairs, although only a minority took advantage of the opportunity to act. Religious belief provided the stimulus for most of those who were engaged in the struggles for a better society. But the effect of a few women preaching, prophesying and writing was a stimulus to others. Being a woman was not a disqualification for being heeded. Even if women used conservative arguments, such as that the Lord chose the meanest instruments to work his mightiest effects, there was no denying the radicalism of women's behaviour. Judging by the quality of women's public statements after the Revolution, the female sex had made some gains in the 1640s and 1650s.

CHAPTER VII

England and the World in the 1650s

STEVE PINCUS

I

'You know that your enemies be the same that have been accounted your enemies ever since Queen Elizabeth came to the crown,' the Lord Protector Oliver Cromwell informed his second Parliament in 1656, Spain is

> an avowed designed enemy, or wanting nothing of council, wisdom, and prudence, to rout you out of the face of the earth; and when public attempts would not do, how have they, by the Jesuits and other public emissaries, laid foundations to perplex and trouble our government, by taking away the lives of them that they judged to be of any use to preserve our peace.

In so addressing his audience, Cromwell was rehearsing well-known and oft-repeated themes. The Long Parliament's Grand Remonstrance of November 1641 had, after all, begun with a trenchant critique of the Stuart monarchs for their failure to pursue a Protestant foreign policy. After Oliver's death, his secretary John Thurloe pointed out that 'James, indeed, courted the peace with Spain' but in so doing he had abdicated his role as *Defensor Fidei*. Ostensibly, then, the Protectorate's war with Spain, begun with the celebrated Western Design, has justified its depiction by historians as a backward-looking Protestant foreign policy.

Other historians, by contrast, have described England's international role in the 1650s in very different terms. By focusing on the first Anglo-Dutch War (1652–4), they have suggested that Interregnum policy was particularly forward-looking, that it was the first manifestation of the bourgeois revolution in the realm of foreign affairs. The war with Spain, condemned for its anachronism, was roundly criticized by republicans and merchants after Oliver's death for its failure to conform to contemporary economic reality. These historians claim that this reality was recognized belatedly by the Restored Monarchy when it initiated a second war against England's chief trade rival, the Dutch, in 1664–5.

By considering English foreign policy over the entire course of the 1650s, occasionally glancing forward across the barrier of 1660, it is possible to reconcile these contrasting images of England's role in the world in the Interregnum. The confusion is a result of the divergence in the 1650s of two hitherto synonymous descriptions of English foreign policy. Since the age of Elizabeth, the English described their role in European politics as simultaneously defending Protestantism from the papist menace and defending the world from an all-encompassing state, a universal monarchy. Since the most serious aspirant to universal monarchy in the later sixteenth and early seventeenth centuries was Roman Catholic Spain, these two conceptions were in fact synonymous. But, while the Thirty Years War might have begun as a confessional conflict, the entry of France into the war on the side of Sweden and the Dutch Republic made it difficult for Europeans to understand the conflict in those terms. In England, the initial resistance of James I to enter the war on the Protestant side, and the subsequent refusal of Charles I after the death of the Duke of Buckingham to play an active role in the conflict allowed those who advocated intervention to continue to employ somewhat outmoded concepts. The idea of a Protestant foreign policy, still identical with opposition to universal monarchy, had become an ideology of opposition. When those politicians who had so fervently demanded a Protestant foreign policy in the 1630s finally reached positions of authority in the 1650s, they were forced to modify their thinking. If the demise of the Nominated Assembly represented the failure of confessional politics — political alignments along religious divides — in the domestic sphere, the first Dutch War, ironically, signalled the end of apocalyptic foreign policy. The resulting conception of a Protestant foreign policy was, in fact, fundamentally different from the confessional alliance demanded by Puritans in the 1620s and 1630s.

II

The victory over Charles II and his Scottish army at Dunbar on 3 September 1650 consolidated the political position of the English Commonwealth and convinced its leaders that the time had come to seek the long-desired alliance with the Dutch Republic. Less than two months after the English had defeated the young Tarquin, Charles Stuart, the Dutch had been liberated from their own tyrant, William II Prince of Orange, by 'a miracle of Providence' – a mortal case of the smallpox. The Rump Parliament's Council of State immediately seized the opportunity and sent a high-level ambassadorial team to The Hague to achieve 'the nearest conjunction' with the Dutch.

Two strands of contemporary English political argument propelled this policy of Anglo-Dutch union. For many of the English, the events of the past decade had taken on a special significance – it seemed to them as if the prophecies of the last days, described cryptically in the Books of Daniel and Revelation, were being acted out in England. In preparation for the Apocalypse, God was urging His people to return to the pure form of government by judges adopted by the early Hebrews. Through God's spiritual leadership, the chosen people would then destroy all worldly governments in their march against the whore of Babylon, the Pope of Rome. God 'is now coming to set up his prerogative kingly power', the argument ran, and now He 'shall break in pieces the gold, silver, brass, and iron,

The Dutch Republic

The United Provinces of the Netherlands were one of the most complicated polities in seventeenth-century Europe. The Dutch Republic was formed as a military alliance to defend itself – *opstand* in Dutch – against the Spanish monarchy. The Union of Utrecht of 1579 initiated this alliance, but it was anything but a constitution. As a result, the Dutch Republic was technically an alliance among seven independent provinces – Holland, Zeeland, Utrecht, Friesland, Groningen, Overijssel and Gelderland – which conducted a common foreign policy. In practice the province of Holland, most populous and prosperous of the provinces, carried a disproportionate weight in meetings of the central organ of governance, the States General, which met in The Hague.

The situation was further complicated by the historic prestige of the House of Orange–Nassau. It had been a member of this house, William the Silent, who had been the hero of the Dutch Revolt against Spain in the later sixteenth century. His sons, Maurice and Frederick Henry, had led the Dutch armies to victory over Spain in the ensuing Eighty Years War. As a result the Princes of Orange had traditionally been elected to the Stadholderate and Captain-Generalship of each province. As the Princes of Orange increasingly adopted the majesty of baroque monarchs, they began to grasp after their political power as well. In a bid to increase their international prestige, and to secure potential political allies, William II had married Charles I's daughter. By the second decade of the seventeenth century, the battle lines had been drawn between the Orangists and the republicans, who were traditionally led by the chief officer or Grand Pensionary of the States of Holland. The Princes of Orange had been victorious in both head-to-head confrontations – in 1618 when the republican leader John van Oldenbarnevelt was executed and his chief ally Hugo Grotius was sent into permanent exile, and in 1650 when William II successfully cowed Amsterdam into submission and imprisoned his political enemies. But after William II died in late 1650, leaving only a posthumous son, the republicans again had the upper hand. Nevertheless the traditionally Orangist provinces of Overijssel, Gelderland, Groningen and Friesland demanded guarantees for a continued Orangist presence in the Dutch polity. In fact, in our period, each town in the United Provinces was deeply divided into Orangist and republican factions.

and clay . . . all former monarchical governments'. In these special times, the Protestant Dutch, who had achieved their independence by means of an epic struggle against the tyrannical kings of Spain, were the most eligible of Christian soldiers.

Alongside this apocalyptic English self-conception, was an identity based upon a reading of classical and Renaissance history. For these people, among whom must be numbered the Rump's chief propagandist, Marchamont Nedham, and its most eloquent defender, John Milton, a republic was simply the most virtuous form of government. In a world in which monarchies allied to extirpate forms of government which were inimical to their interests, an Anglo-Dutch alliance or union was a prudent form of self-preservation. Naturally there were deep tensions between these ideological strands – deep tensions which often existed within the same individuals – but as long as they agreed upon the desired political ends, these differences remained implicit.

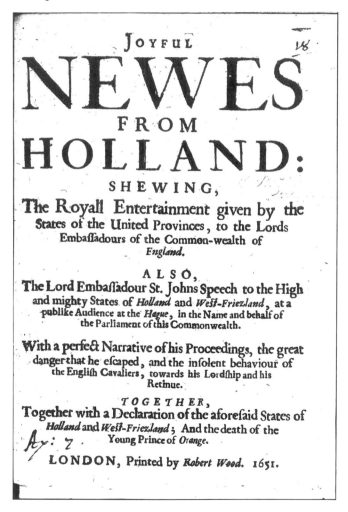

The title page of Joyful News from Holland *(1651), illustrating how the prospect of an Anglo-Dutch alliance was greeted with initial enthusiasm.*

Unfortunately, the much-desired Anglo–Dutch union was not achieved. The ambassadorial mission of Oliver St John and Walter Strickland was an abject failure. Instead of devout Protestants calling for a march on Rome, or virtuous republicans welcoming fellow opponents of tyranny, upon their arrival at The Hague the English ambassadors found angry mobs condemning the Regicide. The English ambassadors soon discovered that the problem was that the Prince of Orange had not been universally detested. Instead, there was a sizeable and powerful Orangist party: 'Orange,' wrote one observer, 'though dead, is still alive here in his faction.' While the governors of the most economically and politically powerful province, Holland, were very much in favour of a strict alliance with the English Commonwealth, the other six provinces had Orangist, and consequently pro-Stuart, sympathies. These provinces made it quite clear that, while willing to accept the economic privileges implicit in an alliance with the English, they wanted none of the accompanying political obligations. The years in the Orangist wilderness, St John thought, had deprived the Dutch of their republican and Protestant virtue. They had become 'juggling sharks', 'a pack of Machiavels which will hear of nothing but their own particular advantage'. Like the Scots, they needed to be reformed by the rod of the Lord.

This perceived Dutch perfidy, far more than the commercial revolution, explains the passage of the Navigation Act in the autumn of 1651. Though it is certainly true that there were members of the merchant community who very much wanted the Rump to intervene constructively in economic affairs, they had repeatedly failed to receive a sympathetic hearing from English policymakers. Indeed, it is hard to understand why, if the execution of the King represented the triumph of a bourgeois revolution, it took the new regime nearly three years to enact such a lynchpin of their ideological programme. Instead it makes more sense to understand the Navigation Act as a piece of legislation intended to punish the Dutch for their iniquity. The Act was written and pushed through Parliament by Oliver St John, the disappointed English ambassador to the United Provinces, who had promised the Dutch at his departure that 'you will . . . repent of having rejected our offers.' It was with full justice, then, that one important group of London merchants recorded that the Navigation Act 'was made when there was inclination to have wars with the Dutch'.

The Navigation Act sailed so smoothly through Parliament because a great deal of the political nation had interpreted the failure of the embassy to the United Provinces in the same light as Oliver St John. Immediately upon the return of the ambassadors, the English presses began spewing forth anti-Dutch propaganda. Newspapers, pamphlets, broadsides, sermons, almanacs and scurrilous poems all drew the same conclusions. The death of the Prince of Orange had not reformed the Dutch. They clearly still sympathized with the cause of monarchy, with the House of Stuart in England and the House

Broadside of 1651 entitled Dr Dorislaw's Ghost: *Dutch materialism and duplicity was popularly castigated.*

of Orange-Nassau in the Netherlands. 'Nor can it be forgotten,' one newspaper reminded its readers, 'how much of monarchy of late crept into the United Provinces, the relics of which are not yet extinct.' 'Thou growest proud and hast forgotten thy God,' the popular almanac writer Nicholas Culpeper warned the Dutch, 'mindest thy self; thy God knows how to bring thee poor again.'

Yet neither the Navigation Act nor the intense English popular disappointment with the Dutch made conflict inevitable. In early 1652 a team of Dutch ambassadors had arrived in England and they were making significant progress in ironing out difficulties by the time hostilities broke out in May 1652. Instead, it was the reality of Orangist political power which initiated the first Anglo-Dutch conflict. The Dutch fleet, heavily recruited from Orangist Zeeland and the equally Orangist north Holland towns, refused to recognize the very existence of the English Commonwealth. As a result, the celebrated Orangist Admiral Van Trump ordered his captains not to pay the normal respect given to English ships encountered in the North Sea: 'not to strike sail to the English upon pain of death, unless they have the Scotch King's colours'. When the English Admiral Robert Blake encountered Van Trump in the Downs on 19 May 1652, the Dutch admiral 'saluted with a broadside'. In the context of the rising tension on both sides, no amount of diplomatic niceties could slow the martial momentum. The first Anglo-Dutch War had begun.

The logic of a Protestant foreign policy had brought England into conflict with the only other Protestant maritime republic. In the context of the early 1650s, Protestant foreign policy meant alliance with other republican states against the combined forces of popery and monarchy. The Dutch, however, rejected this alliance. In the English view, the Dutch had rejected the proposed union because they were still infatuated with the monarchical House of Orange and had become too materialistic to join in the Protestant crusade. The Dutch failure to embrace the English offer of amalgamation revealed them to be, in English eyes, guilty of both corruption and apostasy.

III

As long as the Dutch appeared committed to the restoration of the House of Orange and the House of Stuart, supporters of the English Commonwealth could agree that they were involved in a mortal struggle with the Dutch. It was a struggle which both English and Dutch observers described in epic terms, comparing Anglo-Dutch sea engagements to the battles of Lepanto and Actium.

But, by the autumn of 1653, a series of English naval victories accompanied by a number of adroit political manoeuvres by John De Witt, Grand Pensionary of Holland and leader of the Dutch republican party, allowed the 'good Hollanders' to put down the attempted Orangist counter-revolution. Orangist prospects, which

This tract published in Holland, reflects the distinctly Royalist sentiments of Orangist propaganda.

135

had been so rosy in the summer of 1653, received a sudden and irreversible set-back in August 1653 when Admiral Van Trump was killed in a battle off the Texel. De Witt succeeded in replacing him with a loyal political ally, who proceeded to purge the Dutch Navy of Orangist elements. Indeed the very ships, traditionally called *William* or *Frederick Henry* after the famous Princes of Orange, were renamed after republican virtues. More substantive victories were achieved in town corporations throughout the United Provinces. Town after town dismissed their Orangist councils, replacing them with good republicans. Fortified with these victories, De Witt was able to put an end to Orangist dalliances with English Royalist rebels and to convince the majority of provinces that peace with the English Commonwealth was both possible and desirable.

These new political developments in the United Provinces finally brought into the open the ideological tensions which had been implicit in the original argument for war against the Dutch. The Nominated Assembly, called in July 1653, had been divided from the first between its hotter and more moderate members. The more apocalyptic members of the Nominated Assembly, the political associates of Major-General Thomas Harrison, were unwilling to forgive the Dutch their former apostasy. In these special times, in these last days, they argued, one was either a member of the body of Christ or a limb of the Antichrist. The Dutch had already shown themselves to be an ally of the whore of Babylon. One radical newspaper described the Dutch as 'that viperous generation' which still had 'hopes to suck the Englishmen's blood, which is more sweet unto them than honey'. For John Rogers, one of the most popular of the radical preachers, the United Provinces were to be the first stop on the march to Rome: 'Woe! woe then be to thee, O Flanders full of blood! and Zeeland and Holland full of treacheries! Alas! Alas! weep thou unhappy Babylon!' 'The Dutch must be destroyed,' Harrison himself thundered to a gathering of Londoners, 'and we shall have heaven upon earth.'

Against this onslaught, the more moderate members aligned themselves behind Cromwell. For them, the war appeared to be achieving its aims. The Dutch had clearly felt the rod of the Lord and were reforming themselves. De Witt and his party were to be encouraged, not eviscerated. The radical claim of Dutch apostasy, they insisted, was typical of radical argument by inspiration rather than reason. 'Such a tenet,' argued the Cromwellian propagandist John Hall, 'cannot consist with the very being of a civil magistrate.' Cromwell himself realized that constant appeals to divine inspiration would make resolution of religious and political disputes impossible. Castigation of the Dutch by the religious radicals, thought another moderate, 'will make us stink in the nostrils of all the godly abroad'.

By the late autumn of 1653, the political divisions within the Nominated Assembly had become so profound that government had become impossible. While the violent actions of London crowds suggested just how unpopular the position of the religious radicals had become, their strength within the Nominated Assembly remained undiminished. It was with the conviction that the radicals had lost all popular support that the Cromwellians decided to take action. On the morning of 12 December 1653, the Cromwellian moderates resigned the government into the hands of General Cromwell, who was soon named Lord Protector. Almost immediately the Anglo-Dutch peace negotiations revived. The peace was quickly signed without another engagement at sea. While the resignation of the Nominated Assembly did not put an end to calls for a march on Rome – such calls could be heard for at least another century – never again would those demanding an apocalyptic crusade be close to the centre of power. If political and religious, spiritual and secular elements of the rhetoric of anti-popery had been inextricably intertwined in the early seventeenth century, from this point forward the political element dominated. The idea of a Protestant foreign policy would henceforward be enunciated in language of interest rather than in the enthusiastic tones of the hot men and women of St Anne's Blackfriars.

IV

How did the new English regime, the Protectorate, explain the Anglo-Dutch War which it was now ending? What sort of a peace did it conclude with the Dutch? What interpretation did it place on the idea of a Protestant foreign policy?

A series of publications in the late autumn of 1653 provide the key to understanding the gloss which the Cromwellian moderates placed on the Anglo-Dutch War. The most important of these pamphlets was the first English translation of Thomas Campanella's *Spanish Monarchy*. In this work, originally intended as advice for King Philip II of Spain, Campanella outlined the means whereby Spain could achieve a universal monarchy which would extirpate Protestantism within Europe and drive back the Turk from her borders. The most important part of this strategy, the one which the publisher highlighted and writers as diverse as Marchamont Nedham and William Prynne summarized in print, was to set the two great Protestant maritime powers – England and the United Provinces – against one another. Once that happened, the English ambassador to the United Provinces, George Downing, asked, 'what would then hinder an Universal Empire over our estates, liberties, religion, friends and allies, so long contended for?'

In order to spark the Anglo-Dutch War, the Cromwellian moderates suggested, the Spanish had gained a party in both England and the United Provinces. In England, not surprisingly, it was the religious radicals, those who had been most convinced of Dutch apostasy and most adamantly opposed to peace, who were discovered to be Spanish agents in disguise. Their desire 'to twist the spiritual and civil interest in one', one preacher pointed out, was 'the very Papal and Prelatic principle'. This claim was subse-

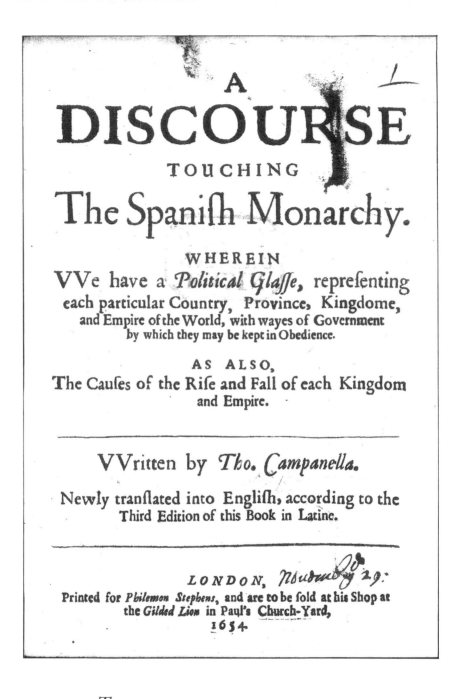

A
DISCOURSE
TOUCHING
The Spaniſh Monarchy.

WHEREIN

VVe have a *Political Glaſſe*, repreſenting each particular Country, Province, Kingdome, and Empire of the World, with wayes of Government by which they may be kept in Obedience.

AS ALSO,

The Cauſes of the Riſe and Fall of each Kingdom and Empire.

VVritten by *Tho. Campanella.*

Newly tranſlated into Engliſh, according to the Third Edition of this Book in Latine.

LONDON,

Printed for *Philemon Stephens,* and are to be ſold at his Shop at the *Gilded Lion* in Paul's Church-Yard, **1654.**

Title page of an anti-Spanish tract of 1654, the most important discussion of Spain's strategy for universal monarchy (especially Spain's plans to trick English and the Dutch to fight one another). Reprinted twice in the 1650s and endlessly paraphrased by others.

quently reinforced when Oliver Cromwell himself revealed that the radical Colonel Sexby had been caught plotting an insurrection with Spanish agents. In the Netherlands, by contrast, the Orangists were discovered to be the allies of the Spanish and the Jesuits. When a packet of Jesuit letters was discovered in the hands of the States of Zeeland, the most Orangist and anglophobic of the Dutch provinces, the Cromwellian newspaper the *Mercurius Politicus* could not resist proclaiming that 'the hand of Spain is much in this war.'

This explanation for the Dutch war led necessarily to an Anglo-Dutch peace and to calls for war with Spain, the viper of Europe. Since Dutch grasping materialism was not perceived to be an evil in itself, but rather to be a symptom of monarchical corruption, the Treaty of Westminster which ended the war did not punish the Dutch economically. Indeed, had this been the English design, they would not have opted for a military strategy which emphasized set-piece battles in the Downs, rather than sniping attacks on Dutch trade routes. Instead the peace demanded that the Dutch exclude for ever the Princes of Orange from the Captain-Generalship of the United Provinces, and that English Royalist exiles should be expelled from Dutch territory. It was a peace which exactly achieved the war aims of the Cromwellian moderates, the prevention of tyranny in the United Provinces and guarantees that Holland and Zeeland would not be the springboard for an English Royalist invasion.

Before the bonfires celebrating peace with the Dutch had burned out, the English began speculating when the war against Spain would begin. Indeed, not more than a fortnight after the final signatures had been affixed to the Treaty of Westminster, Cromwell convened a meeting of his Council to discuss the merits of war with Spain. In this debate Cromwell emphasized that the King of Spain was 'the greatest enemy to the Protestant cause in the world; an old enemy to this nation when it prospered best'. Most of the Council went the same way, only General Lambert dissenting – and his objections were not against the merits of the cause but the feasibility of the design. Rumours circulated on the Exchange, in Vienna, The Hague, Paris, Madrid and Livorno that England would soon attack the Spanish in the West Indies, rumours which were confirmed when members of the Council advised English merchants to wind up their business with Spanish partners. On 20 December 1654, William Penn and Robert Venables conducted an English squadron out of Portsmouth harbour carrying 'such provisions of war as never did any fleet out of England before'. The Western Design, the Cromwellian attack on the Spanish West Indies, had come to fruition.

Pamphlets, sermons, almanacs, broadsides and poems all elaborated on the ideological context of this mission. The Spaniards, observed one pamphleteer, 'are not afraid by public writings to admonish and exhort their king; yea, and to show him the ways and means how he may arrive to the universal monarchy, amongst whom Thomas Campanella is their ringleader'. The author of *The Spaniards*

*T*his tract was the central element in the Black Legend of Spain.
Note the similarity to the Dutch torture scene in
Dr Dorislaw's Ghost.

Cruelty and Treachery to the English in Times of Peace and War pointed out that for the Spaniard to gain possession of 'the high monarchy which he himself alledgeth that he already enjoyeth' he had to conquer 'this isle' and add it 'to the Crown of Spain'. Oliver Cromwell informed his second Parliament that all Europeans, 'the French, the Protestants in Germany have agreed that [the King of Spain's] design was the empire of the whole Christian world, if not more, and upon that ground he looks at this nation as his greatest obstacle'. After Robert Blake had spectacularly destroyed the Spanish Plate fleet in 1658, one poet bragged that 'They who the whole world's monarchy design'd/Are to their ports by our bold fleet confin'd.'

English propagandists resuscitated the full panoply of the Black Legend of Spain. Not only was Las Casas's classic exposition of the Spaniard's cruelty translated into English, but Sir William Davenant set it to music in his opera entitled *The Cruelty of the Spaniards in Peru*. The triumphs of the Elizabethans against Spain were recalled in sermons commemorating 1588, in biographies of Sir Francis Drake and Sir Philip Sidney, and in editions of Elizabethan State papers. The failures of the Stuarts to oppose Spain were also recalled in pamphlets retelling the tragedy of Sir Walter Raleigh and in panegyrics to Gustavus Adolphus. England seemed to be uniting behind the great Elizabethan anti-Spanish struggle which had long been demanded.

But in one important way, it was not an Elizabethan struggle. For the Elizabethans, the main theatre of battle was Europe. By contrast, Cromwellians knew that the best way to defeat an aspiring universal monarch was to sever the sinews of his power. The Thirty Years War and the resultant military revolution had taught the English that wars were won by attrition, not by military genius. Thomas Gage, who went with the fleet to the West Indies as Robert Venables's chaplain, advised Cromwell that 'the Austrian pillar's strength' was 'in the American mines; which being taken away with Austria, Rome's triple crown would soon fall away'. In a dialogue written to explain the justice of the attack on the West Indies, one of the participants rehearsed the commonplace view that 'the treasure of the West Indies is the Spaniard's strength.' Andrew Marvell wished that

> those treasures which both Indies have,/Were buried in as large and deep a grave,/Wars' chief support with them would buried be,/And the land owe her peace unto the sea.

It was because the English had learned this lesson, because they knew to defeat the King of Spain they would have to eliminate his source of strength, that they attacked him in the Indies. Once they had taken an island in the Caribbean, the English reasoned, they would have broken the Spanish monopoly and falsified the supposed donation of the Pope. More importantly, they would have achieved a base from which they could perpetually harass the Spanish Plate fleet.

It must be emphasized that the English design was not an imperialist one. They were not, despite James Harrington's admonitions, attempting to become 'a commonwealth for increase' in order to gain 'the empire of the world'. The English aims were much more limited: they wanted to free up commerce in the Indies for the use of other European nations, thereby preventing the Habsburgs from monopolizing the resources necessary to gain a universal monarchy. The English desired neither 'riches nor private revenge'. The English

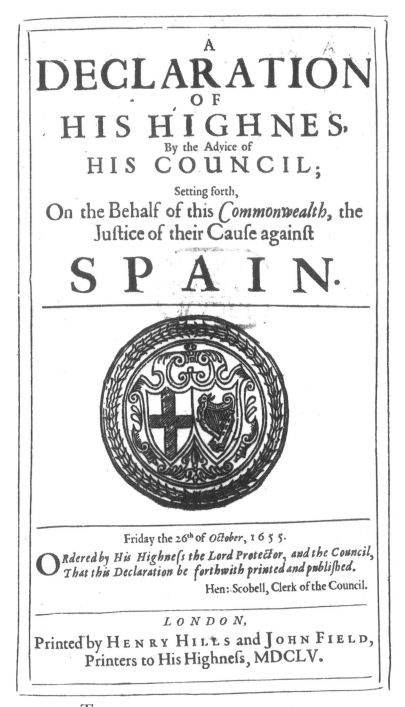

A

DECLARATION

OF

HIS HIGHNES,

By the Advice of

HIS COUNCIL;

Setting forth,

On the Behalf of this *Commonwealth*, the
Juftice of their Caufe againft

SPAIN.

Friday the 26th of *October*, 1 6 5 5.

ORdered by *His Highnefs the Lord Protector, and the Council,*
That this Declaration be forthwith printed and publifhed.

Hen: Scobell, Clerk of the Council.

LONDON,
Printed by HENRY HILLS and JOHN FIELD,
Printers to His Highnefs, MDCLV.

*The Protectorate, despite its similarity to a monarchy, very
much felt compelled to explain and justify its foreign policy in the
public sphere.*

goal, Cromwell's first biographer explained, was 'not to bereave [the Spanish] of their treasures' but rather 'to revenge all Europe, unto whom the jealous humour of the Spaniards denies traffic and commerce unto those parts'. It was for this reason that John Thurloe was to gloat after Blake's exploit in the Canary Islands that 'we had received no benefit from it; yet certainly the enemy never had a greater loss.' It is just as significant that the English also spoke of emancipating the American Indians, who were invariably described as noble savages. The republican Thomas Chaloner, for example, wrote 'of wronged Indians, whom you shall set free/From Spanish yoke, and Rome's idolatry.'

What, then, had the idea of a Protestant foreign policy come to mean during the Protectorate? Far from demanding a confessional crusade, supporters of the Protectorate expected that their government would apply the principles of the Good Old Cause to foreign affairs. These principles, 'the true foundation and ground of this great war on the Parliament's part', John Thurloe explained to Bulstrode Whitelocke when he was ambassador in Sweden, was that 'sober Christians were afraid of imposing upon their consciences and everybody of having arbitrary power set up over their estates to the distraction of all their liberties'. In practice this meant that England's natural enemy was Spain, the land of the Inquisition, a nation which sought to enslave the rest of the world. France, by contrast, was an eligible ally, despite being a Roman Catholic nation, because it had granted liberty of conscience to the Huguenots. 'The liberty which is granted by the French to those who are of a different opinion in the point of religion,' recalled one contemporary, 'was a great inducement to move his Highness to a peace with this nation, since himself was ever so tender in matters of religion.'

V

Despite the ostensible success of Cromwell's war with Spain – England took Jamaica in the West Indies and Dunkirk on the European mainland – the war became increasingly unpopular. This was in part because it proved to be an economic disaster; trade routes which had not been lost to the French during the Anglo-Dutch War were now lost to the Dutch in the war with Spain. Mostly, however, English opinion turned against the war because it was perceived to be anachronistic. Spain was no longer a serious contender for the universal monarchy.

Developments in northern Europe provided an opportunity to re-evaluate English foreign policy. The military success of Oliver Cromwell's ally in the Protestant cause, Charles X King of Sweden, provoked a Baltic crisis in 1659–60. By attacking Denmark in 1658, the new Swedish monarch threatened to achieve complete domination over the Sound, a vital source of naval materials for England and the United Provinces. The Dutch, unsurprisingly, responded by sending a fleet in support of Denmark, in an effort to keep the

The Western Design

Immediately after the establishment of the Protectorate, soon after the Treaty of Westminster was signed ending the Anglo-Dutch War, Oliver Cromwell was able to persuade his Council of State that the time had come to attack the Spanish monarchy, and attack it in the West Indies. Unlike the Elizabethan privateering missions, however, this assault on the Spanish Empire in America was to be the main thrust of the war strategy. While the Elizabethans had quaked in terror at the thought of Spanish tercios on Irish or English soil, the Spanish defeat in the Eighty Years War with the Dutch led to an English reassessment of the nature of Spanish power. It was not their military might, but their economic resources which made the House of Austria a threat to dominate the world. So, instead of harassing the Spanish King in the West Indies and singeing his beard in Spain itself, the Cromwellians decided to mount a full-scale assault on the Spanish American colonies. Contemporaries universally marvelled at the size and preparation of the fleet Cromwell had mobilized. Hispaniola – modern Haiti and the Dominican Republic – was the prime target. Not only was it a large and rich island, but it was centrally situated to interrupt Spanish shipping lanes. With Hispaniola, the English would have destroyed the Spanish economic monopoly in the West Indies.

Unfortunately, the well-planned attack, led by the experienced William Penn and Robert Venables, failed to achieve its goal. The landing on

Sound open. Richard Cromwell, who had succeeded his father as Lord Protector in September 1658, clearly had to take some action. More importantly, the crisis provided an opportunity for Oliver's critics to voice their disapproval of his foreign policy.

The republicans and radicals who had been dismissed from Oliver's parliaments roundly condemned the war with Spain. They did not, however, condemn Cromwell for failing to achieve a commercial empire. Speaker after speaker lamented the Dutch peace and the Spanish war. They moaned that the war with Spain had destroyed English trade. 'Was not the effect of the peace with Holland, and the war with Spain, the most disadvantageous and deplorable that ever were?' Thomas Scot asked rhetorically. More importantly, Cromwell's critics saw the war as unnecessary. Spain's pretensions to universal monarchy were a very real concern in Elizabeth's days, they admitted, but since the Treaty of Munster (1648) Spain had clearly given over those pretensions. The observation of the Spanish merchant, John Paige – 'I look upon the Spaniards as a lost nation' – was shared by all of the Protectorate's critics.

The alternative foreign policy proposed by those critical of the Spanish war was not, as one would expect from those ostensible defenders of the bourgeois revolution, a new trade war with the

Hispaniola was marred by a series of disasters. The ships were forced to put in too far away from the town of Santo Domingo; the troops withered in the march across the island in the tropical heat; and, ultimately, the vital scout was killed at the beginning of the assault. But the English were able to salvage the mission by capturing the island of Jamaica. That island, though certainly not the primary aim of the mission, was perfectly adequate to serve the English purposes. It was just as fertile as Hispaniola and 'lies in the very heart of the Spaniard to gall him'. The experienced West Indies merchant Thomas Modyford even remarked that he 'could heartily have wished it had been their first attempt' since 'this will more trouble the court of Spain than ten of the other'. Nevertheless most in England, unaware perhaps of the realities of Caribbean geography, were less optimistic. As soon as the news was widely known it 'begot a very sad spirit through out our whole island'. The ostensible frowning of Providence soon gave way to more concrete and widely voiced criticisms of the war with Spain begun by the Western Design. While the English might have broken the Spanish trading monopoly, this did not prevent the Spanish from seizing the vast store of English mercantile capital in Spain and the Canary Islands. Coming soon after the economically devastating Dutch War, this blow cut to the quick. More significantly, the spectacular victories of Charles X of Sweden, and the less dramatic but more steady advances of the French armies in Northern Europe, made the claim that Spain was seeking world dominion all too implausible. Even before Cromwell's death, the war against Spain had come to be seen as an anachronism.

Dutch. They were critical of Cromwell's peace with the Dutch Republic because he had lost a golden opportunity to bring them 'to oneness with us', not because he had neglected to seize their trade routes. Far from demanding a new Dutch war, the radicals heaped praise upon the Dutch Republic. Harry Vane thought it was a model of a successful republic. The Rump's Solicitor-General, Robert Reynolds, described Dutch Baltic policy as being full of 'wisdom'. Thomas Chaloner insisted that 'they have been your friends.' 'If we shall engage in a war with Holland so the Protestant cause can be safe,' Colonel Bampfield asked, 'where is there one foot of Protestant ground that will be at peace?'

Instead of rejecting the principles of Protectorate foreign policy, the political radicals rejected the Protector's analysis of European affairs. They accepted that England needed to prevent universal monarchy, but they denied that Spain represented the greatest threat. The Swede, 'if he be master at land, he will soon be master at sea, and not suffer his commodities to come down to the coast', Lambert warned, 'and if he continues his conquests, he will grow very considerable.' Pamphlets, newspapers and almanacs all expressed fear that the King of Sweden was bidding for the universal monarchy. 'His business must be to make himself not only the greatest master at sea,' agreed Sir Anthony

Ashley Cooper, 'but of trade also. He may overrun Spain, Denmark, Pomerania, Italy, and make himself master of this part of the world.' Sir Henry Vane was more concerned about France, 'who goeth upon the most tyrannical principles of government in the world'. Indeed, many people pointed out that the much celebrated Edict of Nantes, granting statutory toleration to the French Protestants, had become a sham in recent years. More typical of current French religious principles was the massacre of the Protestants in the valleys of Piedmont by the French ally, the Duke of Savoy. Slingsby Bethel was so much persuaded by these lines of analysis that he endorsed them both: Sweden and France, he thought, were likely 'to have divided the Western Empire between them'.

The Baltic crisis tells us a great deal about how much the idea of a Protestant foreign policy had evolved by the later 1650s. While both supporters and critics of the Protectorate called for action and dignified their analyses with Protestant epithets, neither could claim to be supporting a true confessional policy. After all, the Baltic war pitted Lutheran Denmark against Lutheran Sweden. Theologically, there was little to choose between them. English foreign policy, all agreed, was dedicated to the prevention of universal monarchy. But, while the aspiring universal monarch in the early Stuart era had invariably been the Most Catholic King of Spain, the new claimants were the Gallican King of France, the Lutheran King of Sweden, or, according to the more conservative defenders of the Protectorate, the religiously tolerant Dutch Republic.

VI

The revolutionary effect of the Interregnum was most clearly demonstrated after the Restoration. While the restored monarchy did initiate a second Dutch war, it did so for reasons antithetical to the principles upon which the Rump Parliament and Nominated Assembly had defended their foreign policy. While the English Commonwealth had gone to war against the Dutch because they had appeared too thoroughly corrupted with the principles of monarchy and insufficiently committed to the international Protestant cause, the restored monarchy attacked the Dutch because their republicanism represented a threat to the European order and their principles of religious liberty threatened to encourage religious minorities to rebel against regimes in which a uniform religion was established by law.

Nevertheless, in other ways the legacy of the Interregnum was more long-lasting. By the later 1650s the idea of a Protestant foreign policy had been permanently altered. Common interest rather than confessional similarity had become the basis for foreign alliances. In Richard Cromwell's Parliament, John Lambert made an argument which would have been incomprehensible to early Stuart auditors. 'I will not judge,' he said, 'whether this be a Protestant war or no, but that which concerns you is a war which interests yourselves. The interest of England is, or ought to be, the great care in this business.'

Henry Neville clinched the point when he noted

> that the Protestant cause or the Protestant religion are different things. When a war is begun upon account that the Protestant religion is in persecution, as in France and Spain formerly, there is a great concernment, and it ought to move us before all things else. There is no such war now, as I take it. But I call that a Protestant interest or cause, when several particulars agree and league together for maintaining their respective dominions.

A Protestant foreign policy had come to be that policy which best defended national sovereignty. In the idiom of the seventeenth century, this meant preventing the acquisition of universal monarchy. The Restoration country member, Sir Richard Temple, thought that a Protestant foreign policy meant maintaining 'the balance of monarchy and obviating that design [for universal monarchy]', a policy which involved alliance not only with

> the Protestants but all who are on a distinct foot as the Portugal, the Catholic Princes of Germany, Dutch, Italian Princes not dependent on Spain, nay the Pope himself, qua Prince . . . united in this common bottom & kept apart from depending on any of those great monarchs, as also that monarchy, be it France or Spain, which is not in a condition to attempt, but rather to oppose the design in the other.

It was a measure of how much had changed that the Restoration ambassador and secretary of state, Sir William Temple, doubted if there had ever really been a war of religion.

The idea of a Protestant foreign policy had evolved as an idea by which the first two Stuart monarchs could be criticized. After the Puritan Revolution had been achieved, successive Interregnum governments realized just how difficult it was to implement a Protestant foreign policy. The experience of the 1650s altered for ever the terms of the foreign policy debate. While English governments and their critics continued to claim and demand Protestant policies, they meant something very different from what their forefathers expressed when employing similar rhetoric. When Englishmen and women in the 1620s called for war against a Spanish universal monarchy, they envisaged a confessional crusade against the King of Spain and the Pope. When their descendants urged war against the French aspirant to universal monarchy in the later seventeenth century, they imagined an alliance with the Holy Roman Emperor and the Pope, an alliance which they hoped would at the very least be able to deprive the French King of the sinews of war.

Further Reading

Introduction

The best surveys of the Interregnum include G. E. Aylmer, *Rebellion or Revolution England 1640–1660* (Oxford, 1986); Austin Woolrych, *England without a King, 1649–1660* (London, 1983); and R. Hutton, *The British Republic, 1649–1660* (1990). The section on this period in Derek Hirst, *Authority and Conflict, 1603–1658* (1986) is especially strong. Advanced work must still begin with S. R Gardiner, *History of the Commonwealth and Protectorate* (4 vols., London, 1903); and C. H. Firth, *The Last Years of the Protectorate* (2 vols., Oxford, 1909). The best introductions to the unravelling of the Interregnum and the return of the King are the long introduction by Austin Woolrych to *Prose Works of John Milton*, ed. R. W. Ayres, vol. VII, *1658–1660* (New Haven, 1980); and R. Hutton, *The Restoration, 1658–1667* (Oxford, 1985). Two recent works offer fresh appraisals of the Lord Protector: B. Coward, *Oliver Cromwell* (Harlow, 1991); and *Oliver Cromwell and the English Revolution*, ed. J. S. Morrill (London, 1990). For some stimulating thoughts on the place of the Revolution in the longer term see the essay by L. Stone in *Three British Revolutions*, ed. J. G. A. Pocock (1980); and C. Hill, *Some Intellectual Consequences of the English Revolution* (1980).

CHAPTER I
The Struggle for New Constitutional and Institutional Forms

The most helpful introductions to English constitutional history during the Interregnum are G. E. Aylmer, *Rebellion or Revolution? England 1640–1660* (Oxford, 1986); Derek Hirst, *Authority and Conflict: England 1603–1658* (London, 1986); and Austin Woolrych, *England without a King, 1649–1660* (London, 1983).

The fullest political narrative remains S. R. Gardiner, *History of the Commonwealth and Protectorate* (4 vols., London, 1903; repr. 1988); and C. H. Firth, *The Last Years of the Protectorate* (2 vols., London, 1909). Also fundamental are Blair Worden's treatment of *The Rump Parliament, 1648–53* (Cambridge, 1974); and Austin Woolrych's analysis of the period between the dissolution of the Rump and the establishment of the Protectorate in *Commonwealth to Protectorate* (Oxford, 1982). A detailed account of the years 1658–60 is presented in R. Hutton, *The Restoration, 1658–1667* (Oxford, 1985).

For the personality and role of Oliver Cromwell, see *Oliver Cromwell and the English Revolution*,, ed. J.S. Morrill (London, 1990); David L. Smith, *Oliver Cromwell: Politics and Religion in the English Revolution, 1640–1658* (Cambridge, 1991); and B. Coward, *Oliver Cromwell* (Harlow, 1991). The nature of his rule is assessed in Austin Woolrych, 'The Cromwellian Protectorate: A Military Dictatorship?', *History*, lxxv (1990), 207–31. There is a brilliant discussion of Cromwell's relations with successive parliaments in H. R. Trevor-Roper, 'Oliver Cromwell and his Parliaments', in *Religion, the Reformation and Social Change* (3rd edition, London, 1984), pp. 345–91. Roy Sherwood, *The Court of Oliver Cromwell* (London, 1977) is excellent on the growing regality which surrounded the Lord Protector.

The episode of the Major-Generals is explored in Ivan Roots, 'Swordsmen and Decimators – Cromwell's Major-Generals', in *The English Civil War and after, 1642–1658*, ed. R. H. Parry (London, 1970), pp. 78–92; and Anthony Fletcher, 'Oliver Cromwell and the Localities: the Problem of Consent', in *Politics and People in Revolutionary England: essays in honour of Ivan Roots*, ed. C. Jones, M. Newitt and Stephen Roberts (Oxford, 1986), pp. 187–204.

On developments in provincial government, see David Underdown, 'Settlement in the Counties, 1653–1658', in *The Interregnum: The Quest for Settlement, 1646–1660*, ed. G. E. Aylmer (London, 1972), pp. 165–82; and Stephen Roberts, 'Local Government Reform in England and Wales during the Interregnum', in *Into Another Mould*, ed. Ivan Roots (Exeter, 1981), pp. 24–41. The most accessible introduction to the British context is David Stevenson, 'Cromwell, Scotland and Ireland', in *Oliver Cromwell and the English Revolution*, ed. Morrill, pp. 149–80.

Finally, three collections of documents are particularly valuable on the institutional experiments of the Interregnum: *Speeches of Oliver Cromwell*, ed. Ivan Roots (London, 1989); *The Constitutional Documents of the Puritan Revolution, 1625–1660*, ed. S. R. Gardiner (3rd edition, Oxford, 1906; repr. 1980); and *The Stuart Constitution*, ed. J. P. Kenyon (2nd edition, Cambridge, 1986). This last book also contains a very interesting and important commentary.

CHAPTER II
The English Republican Imagination

Blair Worden, 'Classical Republicanism and the Puritan Revolution', in *History and Imagination*, ed. H. Lloyd-Jones, V. Pearl and A. B. Worden (1981).

Blair Worden, 'English Republicanism', in *The Cambridge History of Political Thought 1450–1750*, ed. J. H. Burns with M. Goldie (Cambridge, 1991).

Perez Zagorin, *A History of Political Thought in the English Revolution* (1954).

Zera Fink, *The Classical Republicans* (Princeton, 1945).

Caroline Robbins, *The Eighteenth Century Commonwealthsman* (New Haven, 1959).

James Harrington's Political Works, ed. John Pocock (Cambridge, 1977), Introduction.

John Pocock, *The Machiavellian Moment* (Princeton, 1975).

Felix Raab, *The English Face of Machiavelli* (1964).

Jonathan Scott, ' "The Rapture of Motion": James Harrington's Republicanism', in *Political Discourse in Early Modern Britain*, ed. N. Philippson and Q. Skinner (Cambridge, 1992).

Jonathan Scott, *Algernon Sidney and the English Republic* (Cambridge, 1988).

Jonathan Scott, *Algernon Sidney and the Restoration Crisis* (Cambridge, 1991).

CHAPTER III
The Rule of Law

The most interesting comments on the English attitude to law are contained in the best scholarly narratives of the period:

S. R. Gardiner, *History of the Commonwealth and Protectorate* (4 vols., 1894–1901).

Austin Woolrych, *Commonwealth to Protectorate* (Oxford, 1982).

Blair Worden, *The Rump Parliament 1648–53* (Cambridge, 1974).

On law reform, more narrowly defined:

Mary Cotterell, 'Interregnum law reform: the Hale Commission of 1652', *English Historical Review*, 83 (1968).

Edmund Heward, *Matthew Hale* (1972).

Nancy L. Matthews, *William Sheppard* (Cambridge, 1984).

Stuart E. Prall, *The agitation for law reform in the puritan revolution* (The Hague, 1966).

Donald Veall, *The popular movement for law reform* (Oxford, 1970).

CHAPTER IV
The Frustrations of the Godly

William Lamont, *Godly Rule* (London, 1969) still offers many insights into the experiences of the godly. J. S. Morrill, 'The Church in England, 1642–1649' in *Reactions to the English Civil War*, ed. J. S. Morrill (London, 1982), and Claire Cross, 'The Church in England 1646–1660' in *The Interregnum: The Quest for Settlement* ed. Gerald Aylmer (London, 1972) give contrasting views of the godly's success.

Blair Worden, 'Toleration and the Cromwellian Protectorate', in *Studies in Church History*, 21, ed. W. Shiels (Oxford, 1984) and Anthony Fletcher, 'Oliver Cromwell and the Godly Nation', in *Oliver Cromwell and the English Revolution*, ed. J. S. Morrill (London, 1990) discuss the ambiguities of the Cromwellian religious settlement.

Ann Hughes, 'The Pulpit Guarded: Confrontations between Orthodox and Radicals in Revolutionary England', in *John Bunyan and his England 1628–1688*, ed. Anne Laurence, W. R. Owens and Stuart Sim (London, 1990) discusses the godly ministers' disputes with radicals, while C. Hill, *The World Turned Upside Down* (London, 1972) and *Radical Religion in the English Revolution*, ed. J. F. McGregor and B. Reay (Oxford, 1984) deal with the radicals in their own right.

David Underdown, *Revel, Riot and Rebellion* (Oxford, 1985) provides the cultural context for godly reform while Derek Hirst, 'The Failure of Godly Rule in the English Republic', *Past and Present*, 132 (August 1991) describes its frustration; Ian Green, *The Reestablishment of The Church of England* (Oxford, 1978) and Tim Harris, Paul Seaward and Mark Goldie, *The Politics of Religion in Restoration England* (Oxford, 1990) cover the Restoration settlement; while Michael R. Watts, *The Dissenters*, vol. 1 (Oxford, 1978) is an invaluable guide to the emergence of organized Nonconformity after 1660.

CHAPTER V
The Impact on Society

The best introductions to seventeenth-century social history are J. A. Sharpe, *English Society 1550–1760* (1985); and K. Wrightson, *English Society 1580–1680* (1982). But neither focuses directly on the effects of the English Revolution. One has to turn to an older book, C. Wilson, *England's Apprenticeship* (1965) for a clear guide. C. Hill, *From Reformation to Industrial Revolution* (1968) is a source of much lively discussion, but is not thought to be one of the more persuasive of this great historian's output. For landowners, farmers and change in the countryside, the essential source is *The Agrarian History of England and Wales*, vol. 5, part II, ed. J. Thirsk (Cambridge, 1985), covering 1640–1750. B. Blackwood, *The Lancashire Gentry in the Great Rebellion* (Manchester, 1978) is the fullest and best local study for this purpose. This chapter also draws on an unpublished thesis by Ian Ward, 'The English Peerage, 1649–1660: Government, Authority and Estates', Univ. of Cambridge PhD thesis (1989). M. James, *Social Problems and Policy in the Puritan Revolution* (1930) remains immensely valuable and unduly neglected.

For the Diggers, the best description of their settlements and of their ideas can be found tucked away in J. C. Davis, *Utopia and the Ideal Society* (Cambridge, 1981), ch. 7. The introduction by C. Hill to *Gerrard Winstanley, 'the Law of Freedom and other Writings'* (1973) is more influential but does not cover the settlements.

The Irish land revolution is explored in *A New History of Ireland*, ed. T. Moody, F. X. Martin and F. J. Byrne, vol. iii, *Early Modern Ireland 1534–1691*, (Oxford, 1976), chs. 13 and 14; and K. S. Bottigheimer, *English Money and Irish Land* (Oxford, 1971). The complex social challenges in Scotland can be traced through H. R. Trevor-Roper, *Religion, the Reformation and Social Change* (1967), ch. 8; W. Ferguson, *Scotland's Relations with England: a survey to 1707* (1977); and F. Dow, *Cromwellian Scotland, 1651–1660* (Edinburgh, 1979).

CHAPTER VI
The Challenges to Patriarchalism: How did the Revolution affect Women?

Acknowledgements

I want to thank several people for their help, and to note that they will not necessarily agree with the arguments I have advanced here. Thanks first to Sara Mendelson, with whom I am writing a social history of sixteenth- and seventeenth-century women, for her discussions with me over the last ten years; to John Morrill, for his comments and editorial assistance; to Sara Jones, who has herself written on the 1650s and generously allowed me to see her article; to Val Drake, who has kindly allowed me to consult her thesis on women writers of the 1640s and 1650s; and to many other friends, including Lyndal Roper, Anne Laurence, Mary Prior and my students at the University of Western Australia.

Primary sources

Elspeth Graham *et al.*, *Her Own Life. Autobiographical writings by seventeenth-century Englishwomen* (London, 1989).
The First English Feminist. Reflections on Marriage and other writings by Mary Astell, ed. Bridget Hill (London, 1986).

Secondary sources

Patricia Crawford, 'Women's published writings 1600–1700', in *Women in English Society 1500–1800*, ed. Mary Prior (London, 1985).
Christopher Durston, *The Family in the English Revolution* (Oxford, 1989).
Antonia Fraser, *The Weaker Vessel: Woman's Lot in Seventeenth-Century England* (London, 1984).
Patricia Higgins, 'The reactions of women, with special reference to women petitioners', in *Politics, Religion and the English Civil War*, ed. B. Manning (London, 1973).
C. Hill, *The World Turned Upside Down.* (London, 1972).
Ralph Houlbrooke, *The English Family 1450–1700* (London, 1984).
Dorothy Ludlow, 'Shaking Patriarchy's Foundations: Sectarian Women in England, 1641–1700', in *Triumph over Silence. Women in Protestant History*, ed. Richard L. Greaves (Westport, Conn., 1985).
Phyllis Mack, 'Women as prophets during the English Civil War', *Feminist Studies*, vol. 8 (1982), pp. 19–45.
Phyllis Mack, 'Gender and Spirituality in Early English Quakerism, 1650–1665', in *Witnesses for Change. Quaker Women over Three Cen-*

turies, ed. Elizabeth Potts Beacon and Susan Mosher Stuard (New Brunswick, 1989).

Keith Thomas, 'Women and the Civil War Sects', in *Crisis in Europe 1550–1560: Essays from Past & Present*, ed. T. Aston (London, 1965).

CHAPTER VII
England and the World in the 1650s

Foreign policy has very much been the forgotten subject in seventeenth-century historiography. Nevertheless there are a number of important and suggestive works to which the student of the 1650s might turn. The place to begin, as with so many topics in Stuart history, is with S. R. Gardiner's *History of the Commonwealth and Protectorate* (London, 1903). Many important insights can be gleaned from Blair Worden's *The Rump Parliament 1648–53* (Cambridge, 1974); and Austin Woolrych's *Commonwealth to Protectorate* (Oxford, 1983). C. Hill's *God's Englishman* (1971) offers an alternative and stimulating framework in which to place the foreign policy of the 1650s. Another context in which to place English foreign policy in the 1650s is suggested by John Pocock in *The Machiavellian Moment* (1975). The only monograph devoted exclusively to English foreign policy in the period is Charles Korr's *Cromwell and the New Model Foreign Policy* (1975). Charles Wilson examines Anglo-Dutch relations in the 1650s and 1660s in his *Profit and Power* (Cambridge, 1976). The Navy, and much else, is described in Bernard Capp's *Cromwell's Navy* (Oxford, 1990). Much can also be learned about republican views of foreign policy in Jonathan Scott's *Algernon Sidney and the English Republic 1623–1677* (Cambridge, 1987).

Several aspects of England's relations with the world have been examined in article form. Economic policy is analysed in Robert Brenner, 'The Civil War Politics of London's Merchant Community', *Past and Present*, 58 (1973), 53–107 and J. P. Cooper, 'Social and Economic Policies under the Commonwealth', in *The Interregnum: The Quest for Settlement*, ed. G. E. Aylmer (1972). A fresh perspective on the first Anglo-Dutch War is offered by Simon Groenveld in 'The English Civil Wars as a Cause of the First Anglo-Dutch War, 1640–1652', in *Historical Journal*, 30 (1987), 541–66. The debate over the merits of the Protectorate foreign policy is also found in a number of articles, see Menna Prestwich, 'Diplomacy and Trade in the Protectorate', in *Journal of Modern History*, 22, 105–21; Roger Crabtree, 'The Idea of a Protestant Foreign Policy', in *Cromwell: A Profile*, ed. Ivan Roots (1972); Michael Roberts, 'Cromwell and the Baltic', in *English Historical Review*, 76 (July 1961), 402–46; and most recently Michael Roberts, 'Introduction' to his *Swedish Diplomats at Cromwell's Court* (Camden, Sa., 1988). For the view from the colonies see Karen Ordahl Kupperman, 'Errand to the Indies: Puritan Colonization from Providence Island through the Western Design', in *William and Mary Quarterly*, 45 (1988), 70–99.

Index